Simple
GREEN
SMOOTHIES

Simple GREEN SMOOTHIES

100+ tasty recipes to lose weight, gain energy, and feel great in your body

JEN HANSARD & JADAH SELLNER

RODALE

RODALE
wellness
your inspired journey

Sign up today to get exclusive access to our authors, exclusive bonuses,
and the most authoritative, useful, and cutting-edge information on health,
wellness, fitness, and living your life to the fullest.

Visit us online at RodaleWellness.com
Join us at Rodale Wellness.com/Join

© 2015 by Jen Hansard and Jadah Sellner

Rodale books may be purchased for business or promotional use or for special sales.
For information, please write to:
Special Markets Department, Rodale Inc., 733 Third Avenue, New York, NY 10017

Printed in China
Rodale Inc. makes every effort to use acid-free ♾, recycled paper ♻.

Food photography by Lindsey Johnson and lifestyle photography by Tara Donne, SheHeWe Photography, and In Her Image Photography
Art direction and book design by Jen Hansard

Library of Congress Cataloging-in-Publication Data is on file with the publisher.

ISBN 978–1–62336–641–4 trade paperback

Distributed to the trade by Macmillan

8   10   9   7   paperback

RODALE.

We inspire and enable people to improve their lives and the world around them.
rodalewellness.com

To our lil' rawkstars:

CLARE, JACKSON, AND ZOE

＝＝～＝＝＝＝

And the amazing dads who
love them—our rawkstar husbands:

RYAN AND GEORGE

Contents

OUR STORY ix

Part 1

THE SIMPLE GREEN SMOOTHIES LIFESTYLE

- - - - - - - - - - - - - - - - -

CHAPTER 1

3 *Embracing One Simple Habit*

CHAPTER 2

15 *Getting Started*

CHAPTER 3

51 *The 10-Day Kick Start*

CHAPTER 4

79 *Going Deeper*

Part 2

SIMPLE GREEN SMOOTHIES: RECIPES FOR LIFE

- -

CHAPTER 5
109 *Simple Green Smoothies*

CHAPTER 6
121 *Energy Boosting*

CHAPTER 7
133 *Natural Beauty*

CHAPTER 8
151 *Kid-Friendly*

CHAPTER 9
167 *Fitness Fuel*

CHAPTER 10
181 *Healing & Immunity Boosting*

CHAPTER 11
197 *Lean & Green*

CHAPTER 12
213 *Delicious Desserts*

CHAPTER 13
229 *Smoothie Bowls*

CHAPTER 14
243 *DIY Recipes*

- -

JOIN THE MOVEMENT 259

RAWESOME RESOURCES 260

ACKNOWLEDGMENTS 269

INDEX 272

Our Story

With every journey, there's always a beginning. Ours was at Woodbridge Park in Studio City, California. We spent most mornings with strollers and sippy cups and usually a coffee or tea, too. We were the Valley Moms' Social Club, a group of about 20 first-time moms who banded together for advice, encouragement, friendship, and sanity. While our babies rolled and crawled around on an eclectic mix of blankets, we talked about poop and spit-up . . . and dreamed of sleep.

Over the years, we said good-bye to Los Angeles and the moms' group and hello to new adventures thousands of miles apart. Jen had her second child and then moved to Tampa to start a church with her husband. Jadah moved to Kauai, Hawaii, to be closer to her mom and start a preschool. It was an exciting time for both of us but also a really scary time. We both were struggling financially and had no health insurance. Then our new church and preschool dreams began to unravel—and both eventually closed down.

As we embraced the chaos, our meals got quicker and less nutritious. Drive-thru dinners, freezers stocked with frozen pizzas, and cupboards loaded with Goldfish crackers became the norm. As the days grew longer and the years grew shorter, our ability to juggle it all gracefully began to fall apart.

Many days, it felt like the energy had been sucked out of our bodies. We were exhausted and feeling constant stress—and still trying to be the best moms we could be. We began to self-medicate with insane amounts of Starbucks coffee (Jen) and giant bowls of ice cream (Jadah). The more we consumed these things, the more we craved them. Yet even these things didn't give us the energy or reassurance we were really craving. So we kept searching for a solution.

In 2011, we made our first green smoothies—and fell in love at first sip. The fresh taste and instant energy buzz kept us blending day after day. Green smoothies became our healthy fast food. We began making them every single day and out went the coffee and endless bowls of ice cream. Our cravings and our bodies began to change. We went from feeling exhausted and defeated to energized and empowered. It blew our minds that one simple change could make such an impact in our lives. And that's just the beginning. Green smoothies have had a huge ripple effect on both of our lives. Together we have ditched the twice-daily runs to Starbucks, easily lost 32 pounds, and look and feel better than we've ever felt before.

Jen's Story:
EXHAUSTED MAMA TO HALF-MARATHON RUNNER

- -

When I was 16, I became the vegetarian who didn't eat vegetables. I survived on grilled cheese sandwiches, Lucky Charms, and bean-and-cheese burritos for 12 years. Sometimes I'd buy a bag of spinach because it was "the healthy thing to do," and then watch it rot away in the fridge because I didn't know what to do with it.

It wasn't until Ryan and I had our second child that I was stopped in my tracks. Having a toddler running around, a newborn who wouldn't stop crying, and a diet extremely low in any real nutrition was a recipe for utter exhaustion. I relied on double shots of espresso to get me out of bed in the morning and another double shot in the afternoon to keep me going until bedtime. Eventually, even that stopped working, and I felt defeated by my own body.

Then one day, Jadah mentioned that she had been drinking green smoothies and felt amazing. Her excitement was supercontagious, so I jotted down her recipe (loaded with spinach!) and made it with my whole family. We all loved the taste, including my young kids.

For me, green smoothies were the gateway drug to a healthier life. Within a few weeks of drinking them, I felt like a different person. I was eager to wake up in the morning (on my own), bike my son to preschool, and then head to the playground with my daughter. I even had energy to go running—and I completed a half-marathon in 2014, the first endurance event I had done in 5 years!

Jadah's Story:
SLIPPIN' BACK INTO HONEYMOON JEANS

I've battled with sugar and carb cravings all my life and tried every diet that was ever invented. Low carb, fasts, calorie counting, point-system based—you name it, I did it. And nothing lasted. I wanted to thrive and not just deprive my body.

I was running out of ideas for what could be a sustainable, long-term solution. Every diet I tried felt restrictive, and I'd always gain the weight back as soon as I stopped the plan. I was losing hope and feeling tired mentally and physically.

In the summer of 2011, I started one simple habit: drinking a green smoothie every day. I was visiting my Auntie Tutti, and she was raving about green smoothies. She promised weight loss, energy, and that I wouldn't actually taste the greens. *Yeah, right!*

My aunt blended my first green smoothie. I took a skeptical sip. Holy kale! It really tasted good! It was love at first sip.

Within just a few days of drinking green smoothies for breakfast, I was satisfied and didn't want to eat anything else until lunchtime. I had this sudden surge of energy to grocery shop and cook. (And I didn't even like cooking. Like, ever.) And, most surprisingly, the weight I gained from my pregnancy was finally coming off. Three months into drinking one green smoothie a day, I finally stepped on a scale and found I was 27 pounds lighter. Finally, six years later, I fit into my "honeymoon jeans" again!

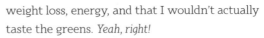

MAKING DAILY SMOOTHIES A LIFESTYLE

When we made our first green smoothies, we stuck with spinach and fruits that were affordable and easy to find. We did what worked for us, and that made us excited to keep on drinking them. The more green smoothies we drank, the more fruits and veggies our bodies craved. It was like they were saying, "Give me more of that good stuff, please!"

We transformed our kitchens into green smoothie stations—the fridges were packed with vibrant produce, the cupboards were lined with Mason jars, and blenders took center stage as the main kitchen appliance. We were blending once a day and trying out new recipes. We'd get a little wild and throw some chard, kale, or fresh herbs into the mix and be excited to taste the results.

It didn't take long for us to run our blenders into the ground—sparks, smoke, the whole she-bang! Yet that didn't stop us from blendin' on. By that time, we were completely hooked on green smoothies. We upgraded to high-speed blenders and made green smoothies for dinner parties, birthday parties, and Super Bowl parties. We pretty much made up excuses to have green smoothie parties to spread the word.

Our friends and family started asking what our secret was. We were beyond excited to teach them how easy it was to blend up leafy greens with fruits. People we love started buying their own blenders, making green smoothies, and getting the same results as we did: lots of energy, weight loss, and cravings for healthier foods. We believe that green smoothies are the kick start to making healthy eating a lifestyle—not a diet.

In 2012, we launched an Instagram account and shared daily pictures of our simple and yummy recipes. Word caught on quickly, and our following grew by thousands of people a day. Since then, we've launched our Web site, SimpleGreenSmoothies.com, where we share even more recipes and host a free 30-Day Green Smoothie Challenge. We've had more than a million people say yes to their health by embracing the green smoothie habit through our community challenges.

It's Not a Diet. It's a Lifestyle.

The Simple Green Smoothies life is as simple as drinking a daily green smoothie. Yet simple can be powerful. We've both done the epic "I'm getting healthy this week" grocery trips, spent tons of money on a cart half full of strange foods, and then been too exhausted and overwhelmed to actually figure out how to cook them. Life was too busy, and we just couldn't get on track to make "healthy" a part of our everyday lifestyle. It turns out that eating healthy can be simple, affordable, and fun—when you start with a green smoothie. We really believe we unlocked the secret to a healthier life with green smoothies. And we're screaming it from the mountaintop!

How to Use This Book

Simple Green Smoothies is the book that we wish we'd had when we first started making green smoothies. It would have saved us from epic smoothie fails, wasted produce, fruit fly attacks, and countless hours on Google. Our hope is that this book helps you fall in love with leafy greens, fresh fruit, nut milks, and chia seeds. The pages that follow are the road map to a sustainable relationship with fresh, whole foods. We want you to experience the same nutritious foundation for health, energy, and happiness that we did—and we're sharing all that goodness right here!

You can read this book from cover to cover or jump around to sections that interest you most. There's no right way to read it; what's more important is that you blend from it. We hope you keep this book in your kitchen and pull it out all the time. (If you happen to get some green smoothie splatters on it, we will jump for joy!)

In **CHAPTER 1**, we'll talk about the one simple habit that can easily transform you from the inside out. You'll also learn about the rawesome health benefits of gulping greens and why we don't count calories.

In **CHAPTER 2**, we'll get you started on the green smoothie journey with basic blending essentials from blenders and leafy greens to the perfect measurements for making a green smoothie in 5 minutes or less every time. We'll also share smoothie hacks that'll save you time and sanity.

In **CHAPTER 3**, we'll guide you through a 10-day kick start, and you'll be equipped with shopping lists, beginner-friendly recipes, and a game plan to drink one green smoothie a day for 10 days.

In **CHAPTER 4**, we will go even deeper and share smoothie boosters, meal replacement options, and how to *really* wash your produce. We have a feeling you'll want to hug us after reading this chapter.

Beginning with **CHAPTER 5**, you'll dive into our green smoothie recipe chapters, where we have more than 100 delicious green smoothie recipes to fuel you before a workout, satisfy a sweet-tooth craving, energize your body, and more!

Ready to rawk out with us? Turn the page and let's jump in!

**RAWKSTAR / ˈròk-stär / : an enthusiastic person
who drinks at least one green smoothie a day**

Part 1

× × × × ×

THE SIMPLE GREEN SMOOTHIES

Lifestyle

EMBRACING
One Simple Habit

*R*eady to embark on a plant-powered adventure full of rawesome results? Whether you're here trying to lose weight, improve your health, prevent a disease, nourish your family, feel happier, get fit, start over, or all of the above, you've come to the right place. We know it can be a little scary trying something new (especially when it's bright green), but we have a feeling you're going to be pleasantly surprised. Our green smoothies taste good, pinkie promise!

WHEN SOMETHING'S JUST GOTTA GIVE . . .

We are all creatures of habit, even when they're the bad ones. But we also have incredible intuition and can sense when things just aren't right with our bodies. We get concerned when our faces start breaking out; we look pregnant when we're not; our arms have a li'l jiggle; we struggle to get out of bed in the morning; we crave the foods that we know make us feel sluggish . . . the list goes on and on.

This is usually when we decide it's time to buck up and go on a diet. We get hopeful that this diet will fix everything, but it's not something we can keep up with for the long term.

As two busy moms doing our best to raise healthy families, keep up our energy levels, and look and feel good ourselves, we were no different. We tried just about everything. Between us, we've embarked upon a dozen different diets in hopes of finding a way to feel amazing in our bodies.

Eventually, we would always give in to the drive-thru cravings or decide that after weeks of consuming nothing but liquids, it was time to actually chew something—and that "something" would be an entire pepperoni pizza. Nothing had lasting results, and we'd find ourselves right back where we started: searching for "the perfect diet."

But the truth is that the majority of diets don't work. According to Dr. Mark Hyman, a bestselling author, a family physician, and an international leader in the field of functional medicine, the average person gains 11 pounds from every diet they go on, because the diets encourage us to eat foods that end up increasing hunger and slowing down our metabolisms. We can't get healthy by counting calories, avoiding carbs, or drinking solely liquids.

Are you ready for a change? Ready to ditch the restrictive diets for good? We hope so, because this is when we get super excited. If you want to get healthier, you have to embrace a lifestyle that's easy to stick with—one that fuels your body with foods to help you overcome exhaustion, sickness, and excess weight. To make a dramatic change in your health, we believe, involves embracing just one healthy habit at a time. Not 20. Not even 5. Start with one *really* good one. Start with a daily green smoothie.

THE SIMPLE GREEN SMOOTHIES HABIT

We're all about one simple habit: drinking a daily green smoothie. This is the first step to making healthy eating a lifestyle. We keep it simple for a reason: because it works. If we complicated things with multiple catches, there would be no way you'd stick with it or progress beyond it. It's easy to set yourself up to fail when you have a huge list of do's and don'ts.

When you embrace the simple habit of drinking a daily green smoothie, you are giving your body permission to transform naturally and happily.

A daily green smoothie is not a short-term program or a diet where you're counting down the days until it's over. Honestly, there's no endgame with green smoothies, just a starting point to a life of health and wellness.

What Is a Green Smoothie?

Are you wondering, "What the heck is in a green smoothie?" Well, you're not alone. People always stop and ask us what the green stuff is that we're drinking. We love the crazy stares! Every green smoothie we blend is based on the following simple formula:

>>> ··· LEAFY GREENS + FRUIT + LIQUID = **GREEN SMOOTHIE** ··· <<<

We embrace the plant-powered goodness all the way! There are a few ingredients you won't find in our green smoothies that you often find in others: dairy, animal-based products, processed sugars, and gluten. We are very intentional about avoiding these ingredients because we know many people are highly sensitive to them and they can trigger allergies and upset tummies. You may not even know you have a sensitivity to any of these foods until you remove them from your diet. Now, are you ready for some leafy love going straight into your body to renew you from the inside out? Oh, kale yeah!

Let Go of Perfection and Embrace the Good

The green smoothie journey changed our lives. It opened the door to nut milks, natural sweeteners, kale chips, buckwheat pillows, organic produce, hot yoga, farm-to-table restaurants, homemade deodorant, backyard chickens, raised garden beds, and grass-fed butter.

We're sure you can tell that we lo-o-ove our leafy greens. But would you believe we also enjoy greasy pizza, extra creamy mac 'n' cheese, hot fudge sundaes, and black licorice? Yep, you read that right. We gulp green smoothies *and* eat greasy pizza.

The difference is, these things used to control us and be in our bodies all day long. We craved these foods and didn't feel satiated until our mouths were stuffed and our bellies were bloated. But that's not the case anymore.

When we have a green smoothie for breakfast, we're just not as tempted to reach for that doughnut later on. So, yes, we still enjoy unhealthy things, but we now choose when we

I eat REAL FOOD to fuel
my awesome life.
I PLAY & LAUGH to fuel
my soul.
I DRINK my
Greens
I dance with my fears. I chase my dreams.
This is MY body. This is MY health.
This is my LIFESTYLE.
whole foods. whole hearts.
For the WHOLE world.

— THE RAWKSTAR MANIFESTO —

feel like indulging. It's like the chains of the processed food world have been broken, and we can say yes or no to junk food without an internal struggle.

A big part of the green smoothie lifestyle is accepting our imperfections, listening to our cravings, celebrating any win (big or small), and sticking with our daily green smoothie habit. Our hope is that you experience this same food freedom we have found by drinking a daily green smoothie.

Why We Don't Count Calories

When we focus on counting calories or tracking points, we forget what truly matters—vitamins and nutrients. The simple truth is that calories are not equal. For example, you can gulp down a 100-calorie soda or a 100-calorie green smoothie. Sure, they have the same number of calories, but the differences in their health benefits are drastic.

The soda fills your body with sodium and processed sugar that spike your blood sugar levels and cause you to crave more of it. A green smoothie fills your body with vitamins A and C, potassium, calcium, and fiber—which fill you up, stabilize your blood sugar levels, and energize your body naturally. This is why we focus on nutrients, not calories.

If weight loss is a goal, you can happily achieve this without counting calories. Yep, we said it! What we recommend is consuming low-glycemic green smoothies, which you can find in the Lean & Green recipe section. These smoothies are lower in sugars and calories yet high in nutrients, so your body will be nourished.

A HEALTHY HABIT FUELS AN AWESOME LIFE

Once you start fueling your body with leafy greens, veggies, and fruit with a daily green smoothie, you'll start craving them more and more—and the rawesome results will begin to unfold. Some results will come quickly, and others will take time to reveal themselves. Here are some of our favorite health benefits that you can experience by drinking a daily green smoothie.

INCREASED ENERGY. Green smoothies give you extra pep in your step. The actual blending process breaks down plant cell walls, making it easier for your body to digest and absorb the nutrients. So not only does your body do less work than it normally would to digest these foods, but you also absorb more nutrients from them.

"It took us 30 years, but we finally crave spinach smoothies, kale chips, and roasted Brussels sprouts. Our moms are so proud of us."

—JEN & JADAH

GLOWING SKIN. A diet high in leafy greens means you are loading up on chlorophyll, which helps purge toxins from the inside out, replenishes cells, and restores the skin quickly. Get your glow on with healthy, happy skin.

SHARPER CLARITY AND FOCUS. The combination of high-fiber leafy greens and fruit gives you steady, stable, consistent energy. Say adios to brain fog and hello to quick wit and focus!

STRENGTHENED IMMUNE SYSTEM. Blending fruits and veggies that are high in vitamins A and C boosts the immune system, which is your body's natural defense system against infections and viruses. Leafy greens support the lymphatic system, flush out toxins, and reduce inflammation.

REGULAR BOWEL MOVEMENTS. The fiber found in green smoothies acts as an internal broom to help digested food inside your body "move along." We're all for regular bathroom trips and less digestive discomfort throughout the day. Over time, regular bowel movements can help with bloating, acne, and weight loss. Holla!

WEIGHT LOSS. Green smoothies are loaded with nutrients and packed with fiber, which all aid in weight loss. Plus, fiber and healthy fats keep you full and energized, making working out even more doable. Oftentimes, green smoothie rawkstars lose weight without even trying. Now that's what we call a happy side effect!

Sick of Getting Sick?

Ever since we started drinking green smoothies, both of our families have dodged our fair share of colds and flus. And when we do get hit, we bounce back quickly since our immune systems are strong and ready for battle. When we feel a little sickness coming on, we've been known to gulp certain green smoothie recipes up the ying yang. (You can learn all about them in Chapter 10.)

Yet the thing we're most proud of is that our kids have weathered the preschool and early elementary school viruses insanely well. They haven't needed antibiotics in the last 5 years—which is exactly when we first started drinking green smoothies. Coincidence? We don't think so.

Praise from Our Rawkstars

As much as we enjoy telling you about the health benefits you will experience when you drink a daily green smoothie, we also love sharing stories straight from our community. These rawkstars are happy to share with you a piece of their journey.

"I feel energized. A lot of days, I even choose to take my green smoothie on my way to work instead of my morning coffee! It's incredible how quickly you can just whip up one of those smoothies. Thanks for introducing me to green smoothies; I will not stop here. They will stay on my meal plan, and I am excited to follow you until the next 30-day challenge."

—NICOLE BENT

* * *

"The best part was seeing my kids beg for my smoothies. My oldest son, who is 3½, has Down syndrome, and he is one picky eater. But he loved these! I'm looking forward to keeping with the habit and sharing with my kids." **—TARA CHERRY**

* * *

"The idea of drinking spinach was a turnoff at first. I have tried several diets and get bored easily. Since starting the challenge, I've lost 10 pounds! I am sleeping a lot better, have more energy, and make better choices when it comes to my other meals throughout the day!"

—AMANDA LANDRETH

"Green smoothies have drastically changed my life! I'm in college, and I have been eating horrible foods, since they're often readily available. I often felt sluggish and had little to no energy. I came across your Web site and began making my own green smoothies. This is the best thing I've ever done! Since doing so, I now feel more energized, and I'm even doing better in school. I have also made my friends into green smoothie lovers. We even have green smoothie parties and come up with new and exciting recipes!"

—KATIE HOUSE

* * *

"I've been trying to improve my diet and the quality of my food for many years. Some days I just can't stand to look at another salad, piece of fruit, or vegetable! I've been drinking green smoothies for the last 9 days. I can't believe how amazing I feel and how easy this is to do. I even get a bigger boost of energy from green smoothies than from my morning coffee!" **—RANDY KIMBALL**

2

GETTING STARTED

We want to share all the things we wish we'd known when we first started drinking green smoothies. Inside this chapter, you'll find everything you need to hop on the green smoothie train—including essential tools, our rawkstar recipe formula, and tips to help you become the next green smoothie rawkstar. This is Green Smoothies 101 . . . and class starts right now!

RAWKSTAR BLENDER GUIDE

There is only one essential tool you need to make a green smoothie: a blender. Yep, that's seriously it. We told you this lifestyle is simple! Start blending with whatever you have (or can borrow from a friend) and you'll be on your way to rawkstar status in no time!

We started blending the greens with our dusty wedding-gift blenders, a Magic Bullet (Jadah) and a Waring Pro Single-Speed Blender (Jen). We rawked out with our basic blenders every single day. They did what we needed them to do—and for a really good price.

Blend Your Heart Out: Choosing the Right Blender

The best advice we can give about choosing a blender is to find one that aligns with your lifestyle. Figure out how many people you're making smoothies for and how much money you want to spend. Our goal is to guide you to purchase the right blender at the right time. Here are a few of our favorites.

VITAMIX 7500: Vitamix is one of the most coveted blenders, and for good reason—the performance and warranty are amazing. The BPA-free containers make blending all of the ingredients a breeze. Starts at $300.

VITAMIX S30: This space-saving blender is perfect for small families or making lots of on-the-go smoothies (it includes a travel cup). Don't let its adorable size fool you—it's packed with power, making it our favorite blender to travel with. Starts at $400.

BLENDTEC 725: This sleek design makes blending your favorite recipes easy. Simply put your leafy greens, fruits, and liquid into the BPA-free pitcher, press the "smoothie" button, and this machine does all the work. We personally love the Designer Series because the touchscreen has empowering, fun phrases every time you blend! Starts at $320.

BREVILLE HEMISPHERE: This durable and sleek blender has innovative blades that'll push and pull ingredients from the top and bottom, creating the perfect blend with one touch. Starts at $200.

NUTRIBULLET PRO: This single-serving blender is compact, lightweight, and easy to clean. Just

Buy a Refurbished Blender

When I couldn't squeeze a high-powered blender into my budget, I bought a certified reconditioned Vitamix in 2012, and it's still going strong! It's our little savings secret that we wish more people knew about. You can save hundreds of dollars, and these blenders often come with an amazing factory warranty. You can usually do a quick online search using the word *reconditioned* or *refurbished* along with the blender brand name you're looking for to see if what you want is sold this way. **—JEN**

Clockwise from top left: Black & Decker Fusion Blade, Blendtec 725, Vitamix 7500, Breville Hemisphere, Oster Counterforms, Vitamix S30, Nutribullet Pro, Cuisinart Smart Stick

Juicing versus Blending

There's are two great ways to "drink" your veggies—juicing and blending. Both help you get your glow on—but it's important to understand the different benefits.

BLENDING: GULP THE PULP. Blending breaks down the plant cell walls, making it easier for your body to digest the nutrients. The fiber stays intact, which slows down the absorption of natural sugar so you have a more stable energy boost. Fiber also keeps you feeling full longer and does a little sweep to get the gunk out of your body. With blending, there's very little wasted produce, and cleanup is easy.

JUICING: SIP THE JUICE. A juicer strips the fiber from the fruits and veggies, which gives you a light, refreshing drink. It also gives your digestive system a break to rest and repair. The natural sugars are quickly absorbed into your bloodstream, giving you a nice, quick energy jolt. Juicing requires more prep work. There's also more cleanup since the fiber is being removed from the juice.

be careful not to overpack the container, which can cause leaking. Starts at $100.

OSTER COUNTERFORMS: This brushed stainless blender is affordable and reliable. It does a good job blending green smoothies with a solid glass pitcher and 600-watt motor. Starts at $65.

BLACK & DECKER FUSION BLADE: This super-affordable blender is a digital smoothie-making machine. It comes with a 48-ounce glass jar and a smaller personal-size blender, making it a "two for the price of one" deal. Starts at $55.

CUISINART SMART STICK: This 200-watt compact blender fits right in a widemouthed Mason jar, making cleanup a breeze. It comes in a variety of fun colors and is small enough to store in a kitchen drawer. Starts at $30.

Same smoothie using a regular blender (left) and a high-speed blender (right).

How to *Really* Clean Your Blender

The easiest and fastest way to clean your blender is to give it a quick rinse with warm water right after use. Then fill it half full with warm water and one or two tiny drops of dish soap. Place it back on the base (with the lid in place!) and turn the blender on for 30 seconds—it's like a mini dishwasher! You'll want to remove the blender from the base and give it a good rinse to remove any remaining soapsuds.

If you're in a hurry, fill your blender with water and leave it in the sink to soak until you're ready to wash it. Otherwise, it will be a pain to clean later.

Deep Cleaning Your Cloudy Blender

Minerals collect on the blender container when you're blending fresh produce, which can quickly turn it into a cloudy mess. Simply add 1 cup of white vinegar to the container and fill it three-quarters full with warm water. Allow to soak for a few hours, then softly scrub the inside of the container with a sponge. Rinse well and enjoy a sparkling container.

Three Ways to Show Your Blender Some Extra Love

1. Cut hard ingredients into bite-size pieces (about 1 inch) before adding them to the blender. We're looking at you, carrots, apples, and beets.

2. Defrost frozen fruit in the fridge the night before or on the countertop for 30 minutes before blending. This boosts the flavor, sweetness, and liquid content of your smoothie. It's also gentler on your blender blade.

3. Pay attention to the blender vortex (aka the tornado) to determine if you have enough liquid. If things aren't spinning around, open the peephole on top and add a little more liquid. You can also use a tamper, wooden spoon, or celery stick to push down the ingredients and help the blades catch them.

RAWKSTAR ACCESSORIES

Before we let that blender roar, we want to share some of our favorite green smoothie accessories (and slight obsessions) that make us do a happy dance in the kitchen. Ain't no party like a green smoothie party, cuz the green smoothie party won't stop!

MASON JARS: Mason jars have our hearts. They are strong, made of glass (no scary BPA!), reusable, multifunctional, and supercute. We use pint-size jars for a single serving, the half-pint size for our kids, and the quart size for storing green smoothie leftovers in the fridge. Wide-mouthed jars are typically easier to clean, but regular-mouthed jars have better lid options.

MASON JAR STORAGE CAPS: These BPA-free lids are great for storing green smoothies in the fridge. Keeping a lid on your smoothie helps limit oxidation. Oxidation can happen when produce is blended and exposed to air, which causes the nutrients to break down over time. If you're making a smoothie for later, seal it with an airtight lid.

MASON JAR LIDS: To avoid green smoothie spills, we love to use Mason jar lids. Cuppow has an opening similar to "to go" coffee cups, if you like to sip your smoothie. The Mason Bar Company has fun, colorful lids, preventing tons of spills. The daisy cut lids add pizzazz to your green smoothie, but they are more for style points than their ability to prevent spills. Combine these last two styles for a stylish and spill-proof experience.

"A lot of spaghetti sauce jars are actually Mason jars in disguise. All you need to do is buy the sauce, use it for a meal, wash the jar out, and peel off the label. Then you have a cute jar for your green smoothies."

STRAWS + STRAW BRUSH: Save the planet and skip the plastic. Reusable straws are an earth-friendly way to sip your daily green smoothies. We love stainless steel straws, which add a touch of luxury to smoothie time. If you go this route, invest a few dollars in a small brush for cleaning the inside (you can thank us later!). For traveling, parties, or when you're on the go, we like to use ecofriendly paper straws.

WATER FILTER: Not all water is equal when it comes to quality. We definitely recommend you invest in a water filter. Jadah has the Brita faucet-filtration system, which is space efficient and easy to install. Jen has the Berkey countertop water-filter system, which does a great job of removing impurities from not-so-amazing tap water.

VEGGIE WASH: Fresh produce is our favorite! Yet this also means we have to make sure that what we're eating is clean (aka free of pesticides, chemicals, and waxes). Keeping veggie wash by the sink makes it easy to say adios to harmful chemicals.

TOTE BAG: Once you have the green smoothie habit down, you'll want to have a cute canvas bag to rawk on your next farmers' market trip. Don't forget to pack in those leafy greens like a champ!

COMPOST BIN: Tired of wasting all of those extra fruit and veggie scraps? Start a compost pile for your garden with an easy-to-carry compost bin that fits easily on a kitchen countertop.

How We Compost on the Hansard Farm

With three large raised garden beds, we're always in need of compost to enrich the soil organically. Our three-step process turns produce scraps into garden goodness.

1. Dump produce scraps into a kitchen countertop compost bin (we compost fruit, veggies, and coffee grounds).

2. Once a day, dump the compost bin into a backyard metal trash can with holes drilled in the bottom and the sides. We used a $\frac{1}{2}$-inch bit and drilled at least 20 holes, which allows for plenty of air to circulate.

3. Cover produce scraps with dry leaves and grass clippings to prevent flies and rodents from getting to them. (This step was a game changer!)

4. After a week, transfer the compost from the trash can to your large compost pile and mix thoroughly.

Over time, the pallet compost breaks down into rich, dark soil with tons of earthworms. We use this compost to fertilize our garden to plant more fruits and veggies. **—JEN**

THE ART OF BLENDING

With our years of green smoothie experience, we've found that the order in which you place your ingredients in the blender affects your overall blend. Hello, smooth operator! Every blender jar is a little different, but the sequence we share below is a great starting point to experiment with and see which order is best for your blender.

Pack: Standard Blender

1. Leafy greens

2. Liquids

3. Fresh fruits and veggies

4. Dry ingredients (spices, powders, seeds, nut butters)

5. Frozen fruits and ice

Pack: Single-Serve Blender

If you have a single-serve blender, you'll want to reverse the order, since you have to flip the jar to attach it to the blender base.

1. Frozen fruits and ice

2. Dry ingredients (spices, powders, seeds, nut butters)

3. Fresh fruits and veggies

4. Liquids

5. Leafy greens

Blend

1. Tightly pack leafy greens in a measuring cup and then toss into the blender.

2. Pour liquid on top of the leafy greens to help create more space in the blender.

3. Add chopped fresh fruit and veggies (1-inch pieces or smaller if using a blender under 300 watts).

4. If using dry ingredients, add to the blender after fresh fruits and before frozen fruits.

5. Add frozen fruits and ice.

6. Blend on medium low for 10 seconds and increase to high speed for about 30 seconds. If it's not creating a vortex, add $\frac{1}{4}$ to $\frac{1}{2}$ cup of liquid to pull the ingredients toward the blade.

7. Pour into a Mason jar (or cup of your choice) and sip like a rawstar!

GOT CHUNKS?

"Do I have spinach in my teeth?" If you're struggling with leafy chunks in your green smoothies (we've been there!), blend your leafy greens and liquid first. Blend for 15 to 30 seconds until you have a juicelike consistency. Stop the blender and add your fruits and any remaining ingredients. Then blend again!

Serving Sizes and Storage

We count 16 ounces of green smoothie as one serving. This means you'll get at least 1 cup of leafy greens and 1½ cups of fruit per serving when you follow our Rawkstar Recipe Formula. With just one green smoothie, you're already super-duper close to reaching your daily fruit and veggie recommendations.

The recipes in this book make two servings, sometimes a little bit more. We call this family style, since we can serve ourselves, our husbands, and small cups for kids all in one blend. We believe that you should share the green smoothie love with a friend or family member—or drink a big green gulp all by yourself. You can also store the extra green smoothie in the fridge for an afternoon snack or save it for tomorrow's morning smoothie.

"Are you an early riser? If you wake up while the rest of your family and neighbors are still sleeping and don't want to disturb them with that loud blender motor, it's smart to make a green smoothie the night before. I store my smoothies in the fridge for up to 2 days, and then grab one for breakfast on the go. Now no more excuses for not getting your blend on!" —JADAH

How to Store a Green Smoothie

For optimal nutritional value, drink your blended green smoothie immediately. Yet sometimes you will have leftovers or need to blend ahead of time. Pop that green smoothie in the fridge in an airtight container, like a Mason jar with a lid. This limits oxidation, which breaks down nutrients and changes the color of your vibrant green smoothie.

FRIDGE: A green smoothie keeps up to 48 hours in the fridge (although they rarely last that long in our homes). Just shake your smoothie well before drinking. Add a small amount of lemon juice to your blender when you make the smoothie to keep it as fresh as possible while it's stored in the fridge. Your body will still reap the benefits of consuming fruits and vegetables even if you don't consume your smoothie right away.

FREEZER: You can store blended green smoothies in the freezer for up to 6 months, but 1 month is preferred. Just pop the frozen smoothie in the fridge at night to defrost so it's ready for you in the morning. Then all you need is a quick shake and you've got a fast pick-me-up.

½ pint
(8 ounces)

1 pint
(16 ounces)

1 quart
(32 ounces)

What's the best time to drink a green smoothie?

You can have your smoothie as your daily breakfast, an afternoon pick-me-up, or a postworkout drink—whatever makes the most sense for you and will help you commit to having it every day. For us, it's having a green smoothie for breakfast. Loading our bodies with fruits and veggies from the get-go fuels us for the day ahead and helps us start out on the right (healthy) foot.

Certain times of day are better for certain ingredients. For example, you want to make sure you are packing in healthy fats, proteins, and nutrient-dense fruit sugars in the early part of the day so your energy reserves are filled and going strong. By dinnertime, your body should be winding down. This is a great time to focus on protein, fat, and lower-glycemic fruits.

"When I start the day with a bagel and cream cheese, I usually crave pizza for lunch. But when I start the day with a green smoothie, I crave salads and soups for lunch." —JEN

To beat the bloat, we recommend drinking your smoothie at least 30 to 60 minutes before or after eating a meal.

GREEN SMOOTHIE
Rawkstar Formula
SERVES 2

It's important for your tastebuds to fall in love with green smoothies at first sip, so you'll keep coming back for more. This starter formula is a foolproof way to make sure you get a delicious green smoothie every time.

As you blend more often, feel free to customize the formula to work better for you. If you're craving greens, add more leafy greens to your recipe. If you think the smoothies are tasting too sweet, decrease the amount of fruit you put in them. If you prefer your smoothies thinner, add more liquid. There are tons of ways you can customize your recipe to create the perfect green smoothie for you, and the Rawkstar Formula is a great way to get started.

2 CUPS (VOLUME) LEAFY GREENS (40 percent)	3 CUPS FRUIT (60 percent)	2 CUPS LIQUID
Arugula*	Apple	Almond milk, unsweetened
Beet top greens*	Apricot	Cashew milk, unsweetened
Bok choy	Avocado	Coconut milk, unsweetened
Broccoli*	Banana	Coconut water, unsweetened
Cabbage*	Berries	Fruit juice (100% juice)
Carrot tops*	Cherries	Hemp milk, unsweetened
Celery	Cucumber	Herbal tea, chilled
Chard	Fig	Oat milk, unsweetened
Collard greens	Grapes	Rice milk, unsweetened
Dandelion greens*	Lemon	Sparkling water
Herbs*	Lime	Water, filtered
Kale	Mango	
Lettuce*	Melon	
Microgreens*	Nectarine	
Mustard	Orange	
Romaine	Papaya	
Spinach	Peach	
Sprouts*	Pear	
Turnip greens*	Pineapple	
Watercress*	Tomatoes	

*These are what we call hard-core greens because they have a more potent flavor that can be hard to mask.

What's a Cup of Leafy Greens?

When we say 1 cup of leafy greens, it's a measurement of volume (how much space it takes up) versus how much it weighs in ounces. So 1 cup of leafy greens to us is a tightly packed amount of leafy greens generously stuffed into a measuring cup that equals 1 cup (8 ounces). Once you and your blender become BFFs, "eyeballing it" and "a couple of handfuls" will become your mottoes.

Taste the Greens

Spinach is the mildest-tasting green, which makes it a great choice for a delicious smoothie. But we don't want you to miss out on all the additional nutrients found in other leafy greens, so it's time we go deeper into the leafy green world. Mixing up your greens ensures that you get the best possible combination of nutrients from various plant sources.

Here's a sweet (or maybe not so sweet) guide to help you put your brave hat on for trying different leafy greens in your next green smoothie creation.

SUBTLE	EARTHY	PEPPERY	BITTER	HERBACEOUS
Spinach	Beet greens	Arugula (rocket)	Kale	Herbs (parsley, cilantro, basil, etc.)
Chard (silverbeet)	Romaine	Red cabbage	Collard greens	Carrot tops
Butter lettuce	Sprouts and microgreens	Mustard greens	Dandelion greens	Celery tops
Baby kale		Watercress	Turnip greens	
Green cabbage			Bok choy	

What's the Dealio with Alkaloid Buildup?

All raw leafy greens carry a small amount of toxins that protect plants from being entirely consumed by animals—and wiping out the plant species. It's a defensive trait, and humans are one of the animals that plants are trying to ward off. If we consume these toxins for long periods of time, they can build up (known as alkaloid buildup) and harm our thyroids. But before you dump your green smoothie down the drain, you should know that this isn't anything to worry about for the majority of people, as long as you occasionally rotate your greens.

"When I started drinking green smoothies, I made the exact same recipe every single day for months: spinach, frozen mixed berries, frozen mango, frozen pineapple, banana, water, hemp protein powder, and ground flaxseed. I never experienced alkaloid buildup or any aversion to any leafy greens in my green smoothies. I actually experienced the opposite. I craved more veggies. I tried new veggies that I never liked before, and now I love them. I also went to the doctor recently, and she said I don't need to come back for a health checkup for another 2 years because my blood-test levels are perfect." —JADAH

Rawkstar Tips for Leafy Greens

FREEZE YOUR GREENS. Did you know you can freeze your raw leafy greens so they don't go bad? We like to keep them fresh in the fridge for 3 days, and then any leafy greens we don't use we just pop in the freezer for a future green smoothie. Store them in a freezer-safe storage bag (like Ziploc) or airtight container for up to 6 weeks. You won't lose the nutrients when freezing them. And when produce is frozen (whether it's spinach, a banana, or a mango), it actually reduces the "green" taste. No more wasted greens!

ADD A SQUEEZE OF CITRUS. With bitter greens like kale and collards, a squeeze of lime or lemon juice can help balance out the taste and add a refreshing zing.

BLANCH YOUR LEAFY GREENS. If you have a personal dietary reason why you can't consume raw leafy greens, don't let that stop you from rawking the green smoothie lifestyle. You can blanch your leafy greens, freeze them, and then add them to your green smoothie.

SAVE YOUR WILTED LEAFY GREENS. Sometimes leafy greens get droopy and need a little extra love. Fill a big bowl with cold water and submerge your leafy greens. Store overnight in the fridge. Rinse and dry before putting them back in the fridge and pull them out when you're ready to use them.

Smoothie Too Sweet?

Over time, we started to think our green smoothies tasted too sweet. Yep, true story! We started adding more leafy greens and less fruit to them to compensate. We call that the advanced rawkstar formula, and you can learn all about it on page 80. But don't rush to this level. Your body will let you know when it's ready for some more chlorophyll lovin'.

How to Destem Kale
(AND OTHER LEAFY GREENS)

××××××××××××××××××××××××××××××××

To help limit leafy chunks, remove any tough stems from your tough leafy greens, like chard, kale, and beet greens. (High-speed blenders can blend these up incredibly well, but standard blenders do struggle a bit.) Destemming your leafy greens also helps remove some of the bitterness found in kale, collards, and bok choy.

Grab the bottom of your kale stalk with one hand and fold the leaves in half with the outer edge on the outside.

From here you have two options. You can either:

1. Pinch the stalk with the other hand and pull your fingers along the stem to remove the leaves.

2. Place the folded kale on a cutting board and cut the stem away.

TIP: You can add the discarded stalks to your compost or feed them to your bunnies and chickens like Jen does!

Did You Know?

Young leafy greens, those picked during the cooler months, are often sweeter and milder than their full-grown counterparts. During the hotter months, the sun turns leafy greens more bitter. We often blend baby spinach and baby kale, which are sold in bulk bins at the local market.

THE NOT-SO-"GREEN" SMOOTHIE

You throw in a couple handfuls of spinach, a banana, and a cup or two of mixed berries. Then you turn your blender on like a champ, shut it off, and pour your sweet concoction into a Mason jar. You just blended your first green smoothie. Happy dance time! Then you pause, look at your freshly blended creation, and say, "Why isn't my green smoothie green?"

Don't be alarmed! Not every green smoothie recipe will have a vibrant green glow that's photo-worthy. When you add a darker-colored fruit or veggie like beets or some berries, you'll most likely get a more brownish, purplish smoothie. That doesn't mean that you aren't drinking a green smoothie. We call them green smoothies because each recipe includes at least 2 cups of leafy greens (spinach, kale, Swiss chard, etc.), not necessarily because of their final color.

Berries are a great way to boost the antioxidant content and mask the bright green color of most green smoothies. Just know that even though your green smoothie doesn't appear to be green, it's still packed with all the nutritional goodness found in a fresh glass of leafy love. Let's raise a glass to that!

Ripe Fruit: Your Blending Bestie

One of the most common mistakes people make when making green smoothies is adding fruit to the blender before it's ripe. This green smoothie no-no can definitely alter the taste of any recipe. You can save time by buying precut frozen fruit, which is picked at the peak of the growing season and frozen. This makes it easy to have your favorite fruits around all year long, and it also guarantees a chilled smoothie.

A remedy for a not-sweet smoothie is to add a banana, but only if it's ripe. That's why spotted bananas are your friends—their brown spots mean they are ripe and perfectly sweet.

Not a fan of bananas? Swap with any of the following fruits:

- Apples
- Applesauce, unsweetened
- Avocado
- Chia seeds
- Dates
- Figs
- Mango
- Papaya
- Peach
- Pear

TASTE TIP: Freeze your bananas before adding them to smoothies; the banana taste will not be as strong. (In general, this applies to most frozen fruits; it's kind of like using ice cubes, but they're packed with nutrients.)

The Whole Fruit and Nothing but the Fruit

There's a great sugar debate about how much fruit should be in a green smoothie. We stand up for fruit because it has many health benefits—including our favorite superstar, fiber. Fiber is your body's internal broom; it sweeps out the gunk in your gut, which is vital for keeping your body in tip-top shape.

Fruit gets a bad rap because of its sugar content, known as fructose. The sad thing is, Americans don't consume enough fruits and veggies as it is. Yes, we want you to be mindful of what you put in your body (especially if you're monitoring your blood sugar levels), but don't avoid fruit as a part of your healthy diet just to decrease how much sugar you consume!

We intentionally skip adding any refined sugars (like white table sugar) to our green smoothies, since these sugars have no nutritional value. We also stay far away from "zero-calorie" sweeteners because they are made of artificial ingredients like aspartame, which is toxic to your body. The fructose in fruit is different from fructose-based sweeteners used in processed food.

Low-Glycemic Fruits

If you need to pay attention to your blood sugar levels, focus on fruits that are low glycemic to help decrease blood sugar spikes. Just make sure to check with your doctor when you're adding or eliminating any foods to or from your diet.

RASPBERRIES	1 cup	5 g sugar
STRAWBERRIES	1 cup	7 g sugar
GREEN APPLE	1 medium	10 g sugar
PEACH	1 medium	13 g sugar
BLUEBERRIES	1 cup	15 g sugar
PEAR	1 medium	17 g sugar

DIY Fruit Fly Trap

Fruit flies can take over the whole kitchen in the blink of an eye—and drive us up the wall. This simple solution works super well.

½ cup apple cider vinegar

5 drops dish soap

Pour the vinegar into a widemouthed shallow container. Add the dish soap; this breaks the surface tension of the vinegar and causes the flies to sink. Place the container near the fruit fly circus.

Why Dairy-Free and Gluten-Free Matters

We meet rawkstar fans all over the world and recently got to know Sheila Kilbane, MD, an integrative physician who specializes in helping families find the root cause of illnesses by using natural and nutritional therapies whenever possible. What we love is her firsthand experience on how avoiding foods like dairy and gluten can reduce symptoms caused by inflammation. That's why we have made it a personal mission to make all of our green smoothie recipes with no gluten, no dairy, and no added sugars.

✕ ✕

Let me tell you about Sara, one of my patients. She was 6 years old when I first met her. However, her story applies to anyone, whether you are 6 or 96.

Sara began life with recurrent ear infections and had ear tubes placed by 6 months of age. Prior to my first visit with her, she had three bouts of strep throat in a 4-month period, each accompanied by an ear infection. Sara was also a mouth breather, snored at night, and always had a runny nose. Her voice sounded nasally, and she had dark circles under her eyes.

The plan I prescribed for her was similar to what I recommend for many of my patients. We removed dairy and gluten; increased green leafy veggies (through green smoothies, of course), fruits, healthy fats, and clean proteins; and decreased processed foods. I also recommended a few simple supplements (probiotics, omega-3 fats, and vitamin D).

Within a couple of months, almost all of Sara's symptoms had resolved. She not only kicked the ear infections, but she also has not had strep throat, a runny nose, mouth breathing, or a nasal tone to her voice since then.

Sara is very typical of the patients whom many integrative physicians like myself see. They followed what their previous doctors told them to do, but they were still getting sick or were on one or more daily medications and still having symptoms.

This brings us back to the best-kept health secret, which Jen and Jadah have tapped into: Food matters.

To state it simply, we not only need to increase the plant-based foods we are eating, but we also need to decrease foods that inflame our systems. Processed foods high in artificial dyes, colors, and sugar are inflammatory.

In addition, certain food groups cause inflammation in some people. The two big ones are gluten (a protein that is in wheat, barley, and rye) and casein (the predominant protein in dairy products).

So if you or a loved one has any of these symptoms, consider not only adding a green smoothie to your daily routine but also decreasing dairy and gluten to see how you feel.

—SHEILA KILBANE, MD, SHEILAKILBANE.COM

GREEN SMOOTHIE HACKS

After blending for a few years, we've learned a few rawkstar hacks along the way that will save you time, money, and sanity. Pssst...sharing these smoothie hacks with your friends makes you look like the green smoothie pro you're destined to become. This is the good stuff—the stuff we wish we knew when we first started blending our greens.

Natural Flavor Boosters That Rawk

Let your tastebuds be your guide. Not one smoothie will please everybody, but we promise that with more than 100 green smoothie recipes, you will find a few recipes that will become your go-to smoothies. These will be the ones you make for your friends and family to turn them into green smoothie converts, too. We're spreading the green smoothie love together one green smoothie at a time! So explore, experiment, and smile!

USE RIPE FRUIT. A smoothie recipe can be completely changed by how ripe (or not ripe) a piece of fruit is. We make suggestions within each recipe on when you should use fresh ripe fruit or when it's recommended to use frozen fruit.

USE SWEETER ORANGES WHEN POSSIBLE. Not all oranges are the same. When a recipe calls for a citrus fruit, we usually recommend using a sweeter orange like a navel orange or a juicy mandarin. The sweetness of an orange can also vary depending on the season.

START SMALL. When trying a new ingredient with a strong flavor profile (such as ground red pepper or fresh ginger), you want to start with the smallest amount and then adjust to your taste preferences. It's a lot easier to add more of an ingredient and blend for an extra 10 seconds than to try to adjust a recipe for too much of an ingredient.

DEFROST. When you use frozen fruits, the flavors tend to become tasteless, making the fruits more like nutritional ice cubes. If you want to revitalize the fruits' natural flavor, defrost your frozen fruit overnight in the fridge or, if you're in a hurry, let it sit on the counter for 10 minutes before you add your fruit to the blender.

ADD SOME LEMON. If you find a recipe too bland for your liking, add a squeeze of lemon juice to bring out the flavors of each ingredient. It's amazing what a difference a freshly squeezed lemon can make.

REMOVE THE STEMS. To help remove the bitter taste of some of the stronger-tasting greens with stalks, you'll want to remove the stems from your leafy greens like kale and Swiss chard and from herbs like cilantro and basil.

Four Ways to Make the Creamiest Green Smoothies

If you like thick and creamy green smoothies, we have some suggestions for you. A lot of times, extra creamy means extra content (more protein, fiber, carbs, etc.) and less liquid. Creamy green smoothies are a great replacement for meals or postworkout drinks. Without further ado, check out four of our favorite cream-boosting ingredients.

FROZEN FRUIT. Frozen fruit is our go-to option when we want a thick and chilly green smoothie. Our freezers are always stocked with a few staple frozen fruits like mango, pineapple, avocado, and banana.

CREAMY LIQUID BASE. The type of liquid used in a green smoothie can change the consistency a lot. Liquids like water, green tea, and coconut water tend to blend thinner smoothies, while liquids like almond milk, hemp milk, coconut milk, oat milk, and rice milk create creamier smoothies.

CHIA SEEDS. Chia seeds have tons of nutritional value and do a great job of boosting the creamy factor in green smoothies. To unleash the thickness beast, soak chia seeds for 10 minutes in water before blending or mixing into a green smoothie.

BANANA OR AVOCADO—OR BOTH! Adding banana turns a smoothie into a sweet and creamy concoction. You can also use avocado to get the creaminess without the sweetness. If you want the most insanely creamy smoothie, use banana and avocado in the same smoothie. It's life-changing.

Want to know how to freeze bananas?

One of the first mistakes we made when freezing our first batch of bananas was freezing them whole—yes, peel and all. It seemed pretty convenient to us. We found out that they immediately turned a dark muddy brown, and they were impossible to peel. #smoothiefail

The next mistake we made was slicing the bananas and tossing them in a container to freeze. Just as we were about to get our smoothie on, we grabbed one big chunk of bananas all stuck together. We want to save you from those common pitfalls and get you freezing right the first time around!

1. Be sure bananas are fully ripe for maximum sweetness—remember, brown spots are your friends!

2. Peel bananas and chop each into three or four pieces.

3. Place bananas in a single layer on a flat tray and put in the freezer until frozen; this step helps prevent a clumpy banana mess.

4. Transfer the frozen banana pieces to a freezer bag or freezer-safe plastic container and store in the freezer for later use.

Pssst . . . if you want to save some time, you can also just slice a banana or two and place the slices in a single layer inside a freezer bag and store them in the freezer right away. We do this all the time!

How to Save Money with Green Smoothies

If you're new to eating tons of fruits and veggies, you might experience a bit of sticker shock at the grocery store. But your bank account doesn't have to take a big dip because you've said yes to your health. Over time, you'll start replacing a lot of processed food items with fresh produce (without even realizing it). This alone will bring your grocery bill back down to normal. But being on a budget is real, so we want to share a few tips to help you save money while living the green smoothie lifestyle.

MAKE THE SAME SMOOTHIE RECIPE EVERY DAY. Seriously, we pretty much buy the same smoothie ingredients every week with just a slight changeup—kale one week, spinach the next; frozen mango one week, frozen berries the next. We buy these items in bulk because the price goes way down—and it makes shopping a breeze.

SMOOTHIE PREP LIKE A RAWKSTAR. Prep a month's worth of green smoothies at once and freeze. Store the ingredients in a freezer bag or Mason jar, and when you're ready, pour into the blender, add your liquid base, and blend! You can learn how to prep and save time on page 47.

SKIP THE FANCY SUPERFOODS. We intentionally don't share tons of fancy "superfoods" because they can complicate a recipe and definitely increase the cost of your shopping bill. So we keep it simple. And we think whole fruits and veggies are pretty super themselves—without the hefty price tag.

BUY FROZEN. Stores like Costco and Sam's Club sell large bags of organic frozen fruit at really good prices. We personally buy frozen fruits at Trader Joe's and Whole Foods, too.

BUY SEASONAL. If you see a good deal on fresh fruits and leafy greens, buy extra and freeze them in freezer-safe bags for future smoothie ingredients.

How to Thrive When Money Is Really Tight

Eating healthy can cost some serious greens . . . and I'm not talking kale. After all, I've been there myself. A few years ago, my family hit a rough patch. Healthy eating became a serious financial hurdle—and we relied on WIC checks from the government to help us afford groceries for our kids. #truestory

With the WIC program, we'd get a $6-a-week voucher for fresh produce. We'd spend it on spinach, bananas, and mangoes.

There's no doubt about it—we struggled to get healthy foods on a limited budget. But it forced us to get creative, and we did the best we could for that season of our life. Below are some things we did as a family to keep expenses low and our health and happiness high. —JEN

- We stopped eating out.
- We bought "new" furniture on Craigslist.
- I stopped going to Target.
- We made crafts out of recyclable trash.
- We ate lots of meals with friends.

- We rode our bikes to save gas money.
- I shopped at garage sales and thrift shops.
- Family and friends sent us money.
- We simplified.
- We embraced the good stuff.
- We made it work.

"Prepping the smoothies the night before has become my nightly habit. Love, love, love the recipes and shopping lists! They made things super easy!" —**CRYSTAL HAMPTON**

THE RAWKSTAR GUIDE TO PREP

Take some stress out of your morning routine by prepping your green smoothies ahead of time! Are you ready to rawk your green smoothie world a little more during these next 10 days? Then the next step on your road to leafy green health and happiness is making your daily smoothies ahead of time. Prepping shaves off precious minutes in the kitchen, plus it puts the kibosh on any other excuses that stand in the way of you sipping on some healthy green goodness.

Here's what you'll need.

- Fruit, veggies, and leafy greens
- Marker
- Measuring cups
- Quart or gallon freezer-safe storage bags or canning jars with lids (widemouthed preferred)

STEP 1: Wash and cut up fruits and veggies. Make sure your leafy greens are washed, stems removed (we're looking at you, kale!), and ready to toss in the blender. To avoid having fruit freeze together into a solid clump, cut fresh fruit into smaller pieces and flash freeze ahead of time on lined baking sheets.

STEP 2: Label a bag or jar lid with the recipe name and date. You might also want to include a note on how much of a liquid gets blended with each smoothie pack.

STEP 3: Measure the ingredients for each recipe and pack into the bags or jars. Remove as much air as possible from the bags when sealing them. If you're using a Mason jar, start with the fruit, and then add the leafy greens last so they are toward the top. This will make getting them out easier when they're frozen.

STEP 4: Store the bags or jars in the freezer until you're ready to make your smoothies. Don't store them too closely together; there should be some air circulation. That will help the contents freeze quickly. You can store your smoothie packs in the freezer for up to 6 months, although they're best when used within 4 weeks.

When you're ready to make a smoothie, remove a smoothie pack from the freezer. We'll often put a pack in the fridge the night before or set it on the counter for an hour before blending to slightly defrost. Pour the ingredients into your blender along with the liquid base and blend until smooth.

911: Time to Save a Green Smoothie Fail

You know that moment where you stray from a recipe and throw everything but the kitchen sink into your blender? Then you take one sip and kind of wish you hadn't? We call those green smoothie fails. They happen to the best of us. We're always taste-testing in the kitchen, which means we have to go out on a limb and try a new combination of ingredients that seems promising. Risky recipe making is our job. We come up with some fantastic recipes, but more often than not we end up with something that tastes pretty dang terrible.

You can always plug and chug, but these tips will get you back to green smoothie pro status in no time.

ADD A BANANA TO IT. Our favorite way to save a green smoothie fail is by adding a banana or two. The strong, sweet flavor can usually mask any mean green machine.

ADD MORE OF YOUR FAVORITE FRUITS. Not a fan of bananas? Smoothie tastes like Bitter McBitter? Add the naturally sweeter fruits like fresh, ripe pineapple, mango, or oranges. We are big advocates of adding enough fruit to make it enjoyable, and sometimes that requires shakin' up the formula.

THIN IT OUT. If you find yourself with a mean green thickie, you can thin it out by adding more liquid and blending for another 10 seconds. Another option is to embrace the thickness, grab a spoon, and make it a smoothie bowl! Visit Chapter 13 for smoothie bowl inspiration.

FREEZE AS ICE CUBES. Now if it tastes really bad, pour your not-so-tasty sludge into ice cube trays and freeze it. When you make your next delicious smoothie recipe, add 1 or 2 "smoothie fail" cubes to your blender. We bet you won't even taste it.

CHILL IT. Sometimes you use all of your fresh fruits and veggies and then realize you didn't add enough frozen fruits to make it a chilled green smoothie. You can add an extra cup of frozen fruit or toss a few ice cubes straight into the glass if you don't want to alter the texture.

With these rawkstar tips, it's time to rev up your blender and make some delicious green smoothies in the next section of the book—which will delight your tastebuds and transform your body from the inside out in just 10 days!

DIY Cube Hacks

Stocking our freezers full of green smoothie cubes allows us to get quick and creative with our recipes and also saves our ingredients from spoiling. So it's a win-win for us and hopefully for you, too. We don't typically recommend adding ice to your smoothies because it dulls your blender blades and also causes the motor to work extra hard, but these cube recipes are the exception to the rule for us.

LEAFY GREEN CUBES: Never run out of leafy greens with this tip! Blend 2 cups leafy greens with ½ cup liquid base and freeze in ice cube trays. Store in a freezer-proof container until ready to use.

HERBAL CUBES: Adding herb-infused ice cubes to a smoothie can transform a recipe. Blend 2 cups tightly packed herbs with ½ cup liquid and pour into ice cube trays to freeze.

CREAM CUBES: Boost the cream factor in your green smoothie. Blend ½ cup almond milk with 2 bananas and freeze the mixture in ice cube trays or muffin pans.

3

THE 10-DAY
Kick Start

*T*he 10-Day Kick Start is designed to usher you into the green smoothie lifestyle in a fun and delicious way. We've created this guide because we want you to drink a daily green smoothie for the rest of your life. The world will be a better place with more rawkstars in it—so let's get you started on this world-changing habit!

SECRET SAUCE TO FORMING A NEW HABIT

Unfortunately, good intentions alone won't make a habit stick, even a really good one. Luckily, we've found what does work for us, our kids, our husbands—and more than a million people who've become green smoothie rawkstars through our quarterly green smoothie challenges. We've found two common themes among those who've made it to rawkstar status.

1. **A REASON TO MAKE THIS HABIT A PRIORITY:** Choose a powerful "why" behind a daily green smoothie. This will be a game changer. Why do you *really* want to do this? Jot down tangible, specific reasons in a journal or on a sheet of paper and post it on your fridge, in the bathroom, or wherever you can make sure these reasons are seen by you in moments of weakness. Here are some examples to get you started: energy to chase after your kids, get off the high blood pressure medications, fit into your prebaby jeans, encourage your husband and kids to eat better, stop getting sick, etc. Honor your reason to stay committed to the 10 days—and beyond!

2. **A PLAN THAT'S REALISTIC:** We are big believers in having a plan to produce amazing results. It's how we've been able to travel around Europe in the summer, feed our families delicious and nutritious dinners, and get the kids to school on time in the morning. All of these require a plan—and so does becoming the next green smoothie rawkstar. The good news is we have you covered for the 10-Day Kick Start; we'll supply you with a game plan that includes shopping lists, specific recipes, and motivation every single day. Oh, kale yeah! We really want you to succeed.

"I've lost around 3 pounds and quite a few inches, all thanks to green smoothies. My fiancé and I used to be on the all-carbs-all-the-time plan, and now we can't go a day without a green smoothie." —**EMILY SHELL**

THE 10-DAY KICK START GAME PLAN

Wherever you are on your health journey, the 10-Day Kick Start will take you even further. It's time to rawk out with us and give your body some extra love! For the next 10 days, we challenge you to . . .

Drink a Daily Green Smoothie

You don't need to change any other part of your diet or activities—yet. It's really important to focus on one healthy habit before you try to add in another one. That's our recipe for success— keepin' it simple. So yes, we're giving you permission to drink a daily green smoothie *and* visit the drive-thru at your local fast-food joint if you want to. The truth is, that's exactly how we got started on this plant-powered journey.

Get Shopping!

Investing in our health has been one of the most empowering things we've ever done. And it never gets old! Our hearts still melt when we look at our grocery baskets full of fresh, colorful produce. It's like eating a rainbow—and who doesn't want a piece of that?

Three things you should know before you shop:

1. **WE'VE SPLIT THE 10-DAY SHOPPING LIST INTO TWO LISTS (5 DAYS EACH).** This will prevent your produce from going bad. There's nothing enjoyable about opening a bag of rancid spinach—bleh!

2. **OUR SHOPPING LISTS AND RECIPES MAKE ENOUGH FOR TWO PEOPLE.** We encourage you to invite a loved one to join you on this 10-Day Kick Start or to drink a second smoothie every day as a booster. You can also divide the shopping list and recipes in half to serve one or double as needed to serve your entire family.

3. **THE RECIPES AND SHOPPING LISTS ARE HERE TO INSPIRE YOU.** If you have food sensitivities or trouble finding certain ingredients, feel free to get creative and tweak the recipes and shopping lists to work best for you.

Shopping Lists

DAYS 1-5

Produce

- Bananas: 5
- Blueberries (fresh or frozen): ³⁄₄ cup
- Cherries (fresh or frozen): 1 cup
- Mango (fresh or frozen): 3 cups
- Oranges (navel size): 3
- Pineapple (fresh or frozen): 2 cups
- Spinach (fresh): 10 cups (10 ounces)
- Strawberries (fresh or frozen): 2³⁄₄ cups

Liquid

- Almond milk, unsweetened: 4 cups (32 ounces)
- Coconut water, unsweetened: 2 cups (16 ounces)

DAYS 6–10

Produce

- Avocado: 1
- Bananas: 3
- Berries (raspberries, blueberries, blackberries): 1 cup
- Carrot: 1
- Grapes: 3 cups
- Mango (fresh or frozen): 1 cup
- Oranges (navel-size): 1
- Peaches (fresh or frozen): 1 cup
- Pineapple (fresh or frozen): 2 cups
- Spinach (fresh): 10 cups (10 ounces)
- Strawberries (fresh or frozen): 1 cup

Liquid

- Almond milk, unsweetened: 2 cups (16 ounces)
- Coconut water, unsweetened: 3 cups (24 ounces)

----- rawkstar tip

Clean your blender immediately after you make your smoothie for the easiest cleaning. When blending almond butter or other sticky ingredients, be prepared to get out a gentle scrub brush to get your blender squeaky clean.

"Yesterday is gone. Tomorrow has not yet come.
We have only today. Let us begin."

—MOTHER TERESA

✕✕✕✕✕✕✕✕✕✕✕✕✕✕ DAY ONE ✕✕✕✕✕✕✕✕✕✕✕✕✕✕✕✕

We're kicking off this rawkstar party with our all-time favorite recipe. Yes, this is the best green smoothie recipe we've ever created, and we still wake up craving it after all these years! Ready for your first delicious plant-powered green smoothie? May today be the beginning of a new phase in your life—where health and happiness take center stage.

BEGINNER'S *Luck*   SERVES 2

Enjoy this tropical treat full of iron, potassium, and vitamin C galore. This green smoothie is likely to make your tastebuds crave seconds!

2 cups spinach
2 cups water
1 cup chopped mango ✳
1 cup chopped pineapple ✳
2 bananas ✳

1. Blend the spinach and water until smooth.

2. Add the mango, pineapple, and bananas and blend again.

did you know?

Combining vitamin A–rich spinach with vitamin C–rich pineapple aids in the absorption of both vitamins. Vitamin A repairs skin cells, which helps you get that gorgeous glowing skin. Vitamin C is essential for collagen production, which keeps your skin firm and toned. It also supports a healthy metabolism and is an immune-boosting vitamin superhero.

✳ **Use at least one frozen fruit to make a cold green smoothie.**

BEGINNER'S LUCK *Seven Ways*

We want to share with you how we doctor up a recipe. It's easy to make swaps and ingredient add-ons so that any of our green smoothie recipes suit your palate and desired results. Each recipe below makes 2 servings.

MEAL REPLACEMENT

2 cups fresh spinach

2 cups water

1 cup chopped mango

1 cup chopped pineapple

2 bananas

2 tablespoons almond meal

2 tablespoons coconut oil or sliced avocado

PREWORKOUT

2 cups fresh spinach

2 cups coconut water

1 cup chopped mango

1 cup chopped pineapple

2 bananas

2 tablespoons hemp hearts

HERBAL INFUSION

2 cups fresh spinach

2 cups water

1 cup chopped mango

1 cup chopped pineapple

2 bananas

$\frac{1}{4}$ cup chopped fresh basil, mint, or cilantro

BANANA-FREE

2 cups fresh spinach

2 cups water

2 cups chopped mango

1 cup chopped pineapple

LEAFY GREEN CHANGE-UP

2 cups fresh kale

2 cups water

1 cup chopped mango

1 cup chopped pineapple

2 bananas

LESS FRUIT, MORE LEAFY GREENS

3 cups fresh spinach

2 cups water

$\frac{1}{2}$ cup chopped mango

$\frac{1}{2}$ cup chopped pineapple

1 banana

SPICED UP

2 cups fresh spinach

2 cups water

1 cup chopped mango

1 cup chopped pineapple

2 bananas

1 piece ($\frac{1}{2}$") fresh ginger, peeled

DAILY INSPIRATION
· · · · · · · · · · · ·

"Let food be thy medicine. And medicine be thy food."

—Hippocrates

DAY TWO

Are you feeling the plant-powered goodness yet? Gulping 2 cups of leafy greens plus fresh fruit will give you energy you didn't know you had. We usually notice a healthy surge of energy 30 minutes after we drink a smoothie (once the fruit sugars and nutrients are absorbed into the body). That's what we call a natural high!

PINK *Flamango*   SERVES 2

This creamy, strawberry-packed smoothie was the talk of the town for our January 30-Day Green Smoothie Challenge. The sweet mango pairs nicely with the strawberries to balance the insoluble fiber and adds the amazing cream factor.

2 cups spinach
2 cups unsweetened almond milk
2 cups strawberries ✳
1 cup chopped mango ✳

1. Blend the spinach and almond milk until smooth.

2. Add the strawberries and mango and blend again.

did you know?

Almond milk has great flavor, making it our go-to milk alternative. The key to getting store-bought almond milk is to make sure you buy the unsweetened version, which contains less sugar and additives.

rawstar tip

Fresh, ripe berries provide the most flavor, but frozen will work, too. We suggest putting frozen berries in a bowl overnight in the fridge to defrost the sweet juices before you blend them up.

rawstar tip

Removing the pits from fresh cherries can be a bit tedious and messy. We opt for buying the fruit frozen so the pits are already removed. Do what works best for you when it comes to a recipe. #judgementfreezone

"If it doesn't challenge you, it doesn't change you."

—FRED DEVITO

× × × × × × × × × × × × × # DAY THREE × × × × × × × × × × × × × ×

When we first started getting our green smoothie groove on, we messed up a lot. We've thrown in whole oranges (thinking we'd save time by not peeling them first) and ended up gagging down a zesty green smoothie. No matter what we gagged down, we kept on going. Maybe you've already had some memorable moments, or maybe they're coming your way soon. Either way, we're right there with you. Carry on, rawkstar!

PINEAPPLE *Dream Cake*   SERVES 2

This sweet and creamy green smoothie packs a punch with a bowlful of antioxidant-rich cherries. Bananas are great mood boosters, thanks to their high levels of tryptophan, which is converted into serotonin (aka the happy chemical).

2 cups spinach
2 cups unsweetened almond milk
1 cup chopped pineapple ✳
1 cup cherries, pitted ✳
1 banana ✳

1. Blend the spinach and almond milk until smooth.

2. Add the pineapple, cherries, and banana and blend again.

did you know?

Cherries are bursting with antioxidants that help prevent UV skin damage and naturally reverse signs of aging by blocking wrinkles, reducing skin redness, and repairing skin tissue. The pigment molecule anthocyanin is found in cherries and helps keep skin firm, strong, and radiant.

*"What lies behind you and what lies in front of you,
pales in comparison to what lies inside of you."*

—RALPH WALDO EMERSON

DAY FOUR

We are big believers in celebrating accomplishments with words of affirmation, special treats, and midday dance parties. So today, we would love for you to join us in celebrating the fact that you've been gulping the greens for 4 days in a row! Wowza—that's a whole lotta spinach!

VERY *Berry Citrus*   SERVES 2

This little gem is what got us (and our kids) hooked on green smoothies in the beginning! It's full of iron, potassium, vitamin C, and antioxidants, just to name a few of the goodies.

2 cups spinach
2 oranges, peeled
¾ cup water
¾ cup strawberries ✳
¾ cup blueberries ✳
1 banana ✳

1. Blend the spinach, oranges, and water until smooth.

2. Add the strawberries, blueberries, and banana and blend again.

did you know?

Water makes up about 60 percent of our body weight and helps with nutrient absorption, flushes toxins out of our organs, and hydrates our tissues and cells. Aim to drink at least eight 8-ounce glasses of water a day to keep your body rawkin'.

rawkstar tip

A handful of spinach is close to 1 cup measured out. To speed up the blending process, feel free to measure your spinach by the handful rather than using a measuring cup. That's how we roll.

rawstar tip

If fresh oranges are hard to come by (or time is of the essence), feel free to swap a whole orange for ½ cup of orange juice. The best orange juices are those that are 100 percent organic, high in pulp, and not from concentrate.

"Start by doing what's necessary; then do what's possible; and suddenly you're doing the impossible."

—FRANCIS OF ASSISI

✕ ✕ ✕ ✕ ✕ ✕ ✕ ✕ ✕ ✕ ✕ ✕ ✕ ✕ DAY FIVE ✕ ✕ ✕ ✕ ✕ ✕ ✕ ✕ ✕ ✕ ✕ ✕ ✕ ✕

Have you heard the saying "It's more mental than physical"? Some green smoothie recipes aren't gonna sit well with your tastebuds (it's bound to happen!). Yet don't get discouraged and give up—blend on, my friend. Tweak the recipes, create your own, or even plug your nose and gulp it down! You got this and we're right here cheering you on!

MANGO *Orange Madness* SERVES 2

Glowing skin and a stronger immune system are around the corner when you're sippin' on this smoothie that's packed with vitamins A and C. Coconut water is high in potassium, which helps with muscle cramping—making this smoothie a great postworkout one as well.

2 cups spinach

2 cups unsweetened coconut water

1 orange, peeled

1 cup chopped mango ✳

1 banana ✳

1. Blend the spinach, coconut water, and orange until smooth.

2. Add the mango and banana and blend again.

did you know?

Coconut water tastes nothing like coconut! It has more of a salty melon flavor, which was an acquired taste for both of us (but worth it!). This anti-inflammatory, naturally cooling drink does the body some serious good. Coconut water is often called nature's Gatorade, thanks to its unique combo of B vitamins, vitamin C, and potassium.

*"Keep your face towards the sunshine,
and shadows will fall behind you."*

—WALT WHITMAN

× × × × × × × × × × × × × × × × × × # DAY SIX × × × × × × × × × × × × × × × × ×

You're halfway there! When you focus your attention on embracing the good stuff—or, in this case, the "green stuff"—the not-so-great stuff tends to fall by the wayside. So keep gulping the greens, and a healthier life is yours to live. To celebrate, today's recipe is extra decadent and creamy. Let's raise our glasses to that goodness and say, "Cheers to our health!"

CREAM MACHINE *Green Smoothie*   SERVES 2

There is a ton of green goodness found in avocado and spinach, which give you a nice boost of folate and vitamin E. The mango-and-banana combo is a great way to create a creamy, tropical kick.

2 cups spinach

2 cups water

1 avocado, halved, pitted, and peeled

1 cup chopped mango ✱

1 banana ✱

1. Blend the spinach and water until smooth.

2. Add the avocado, mango, and banana and blend again.

did you know?

Avocado is one of the top beauty foods because it moisturizes your skin from the inside out. Avocado is high in healthy fats and rich in vitamin E and B vitamins like niacin, which keep skin cells strong and hydrated and reduce redness.

rawstar tip - - - - - - - - - - - - - - -

Trying to get loved ones to join you on the green
smoothie bandwagon? For the picky eaters, you
may need to skip telling them that there are leafy
greens in there and serve the smoothie in a
concealed cup with a straw. *Shhh*, we won't tell
anybody. It can be our little secret.

- -

rawkstar tip

We recommend you toss aging spinach in the blender with a little water. Once blended, pour into ice cube trays and freeze. We use these as backup greens when we run out of fresh spinach.

"You don't have to eat less. You just have to eat better."

—JADAH AND JEN

XXXXXXXXXXXXX # DAY SEVEN XXXXXXXXXXXXX

We bet you're becoming a ninja with that blender! And you probably see why we call green smoothies the healthiest fast food on earth. You just can't make, consume, and clean up a healthy meal any faster than a green smoothie. #justafact

PEACH *Coconut Dream*   SERVES 2

This sweet, refreshing treat is an antiaging tonic in disguise. The rawstar ingredient is grapes, which offer a heavy dose of resveratrol that slows down the aging process of our cells.

2 cups spinach

1 cup unsweetened coconut
   water

2 cups grapes *

1 cup sliced peaches *

1. Blend the spinach, coconut water, and grapes until smooth.

2. Add the peaches and blend again.

did you know?

Peaches are high in beta-carotene (just like carrots!) and vitamin C, making them one of the most rawesome free-radical fighters in the produce section. Peach power all the way! So what does this really mean for you? Well, vitamin C is essential for the production of healthy collagen, which keeps your skin smooth and youthful.

*"When you are grateful, fear disappears
and abundance appears."*

—TONY ROBBINS

XXXXXXXXXXXXX DAY EIGHT XXXXXXXXXXXXXX

We want you to spend some time today giving thanks for the goodness *and* the challenges in your life. Yep, we've noticed that the more we practice gratitude, the more thankful and content we are with our circumstances, relationships, faith, bodies, and finances. We've had our fair share of struggles and hardships that were crushing. Yet whenever we come out of the other side of that dark tunnel, we find ourselves stronger and wiser than we were before. And for that, we are thankful.

STRAWBERRY *Carrot Cooler*   SERVES 2

Carrots are a sneaky way to add more veggies to your smoothie. Yet the health benefits are fabulous, thanks to their high dose of vitamin A, which keeps your skin, hair, and eyes lookin' good.

2 cups spinach
2 cups unsweetened coconut water
1 cup chopped carrot
1 cup strawberries *
1 cup chopped pineapple *

1. Blend the spinach and coconut water until smooth.

2. Add the carrot, strawberries, and pineapple and blend again.

did you know?

We should all be screaming "yes to carrots!" This vibrant root vegetable is a powerful beauty food that we need to be noshing on constantly if we want to drink from the fountain of youth. Let us explain: Carrots are naturally high in beta-carotene. When you consume beta-carotene, your body converts it into vitamin A and then gets to work.

rawstar tip

Blender isn't keen on blending root vegetables? Lightly steam the carrot the night before and store it in the fridge until you're ready to blend. This will soften it up and give your smoothie a fabulous creamy texture.

rawkstar tip

Not a fan of berry seeds? Blend the berries and your liquid base together first. Then pour this liquid through a mesh sieve. Pour back into the blender, add the remaining ingredients, and blend again.

*"Take care of your body.
It's the only place you have to live in."*

—JIM ROHN

× × × × × × × × × × × × × # DAY NINE × × × × × × × × × × × × × ×

When we started drinking green smoothies, we wanted to work out. It was something we desired and finally had the energy to do. Now, between the two of us, we do dancing, yoga, running, kettlebells, boxing, jumping rope, and biking. Working out makes us feel stronger, confident, and more alive. Green smoothies are the rawstar fuel that gets our bodies moving. How will you move today?

BANANA *Berry Blast* SERVES 2

Oh, this smoothie is a good one! It's full of iron, potassium, and vitamin C. Use prepackaged mixed berries or pick your favorites. With the addition of berries, you'll get a more red or purple hue that makes this recipe picky-eater approved.

2 cups spinach

2 cups unsweetened almond milk

1 cup berries (such as blueberries, raspberries, blackberries) ✱

2 bananas ✱

1. Blend the spinach and almond milk until smooth.

2. Add the berries and bananas and blend again.

did you know?

Bananas are one of our favorite fruits to add to green smoothies. They are a natural sweetener and up the cream factor by a gazillion. But that's not all—bananas pack a punch with potassium, amino acids, and complex carbs. So blend up some bananas and you'll have younger-looking skin, a healthy gut, and energy galore. Start peeling!

xxxxxxxxxxxxxxxxxxxxx # DAY TEN xxxxxxxxxxxxxxxxxxxxxx

You did it! Virtual hugs are happening right now. Here's a little secret: We totally knew you would make it, rawkstar! You're amazing, and we hope this 10-Day Kick Start just reinforced that for you. Now that you have 10 days of green smoothie goodness under your belt, we hope you celebrate this very moment . . . and then keep on going!

CITRUS *Crush*   SERVES 2

This dreamy treat gets a vitamin C boost from the citrus, which helps your body better absorb the rawesome iron from the spinach. Now that's what we call teamwork!

2 cups spinach
1½ cups water
1 orange, peeled
1 cup grapes ✳
1 cup chopped pineapple ✳

1. Blend the spinach, water, and orange until smooth.

2. Add the grapes and pineapple and blend again.

did you know?

Spinach and kale both made the Environmental Working Group's Dirty Dozen Plus list, which means they contained a number of different pesticide residues and showed high concentrations of pesticides relative to other produce items. We recommend you make buying organic leafy greens a priority if it fits into your budget—then your body doesn't have to work so hard flushing out pesticides from conventional produce.

Don't Let Day 10 Be Your Last

You made it 10 days, and we're so happy for you! Now, keep on blending a daily green smoothie! Don't stop after day 10; you have the rest of your life to wake up every day feeling transformed from the inside out. By now, you know what 10 days of drinking green smoothies feels like. Just imagine what 365 days of green smoothies will do for your body!

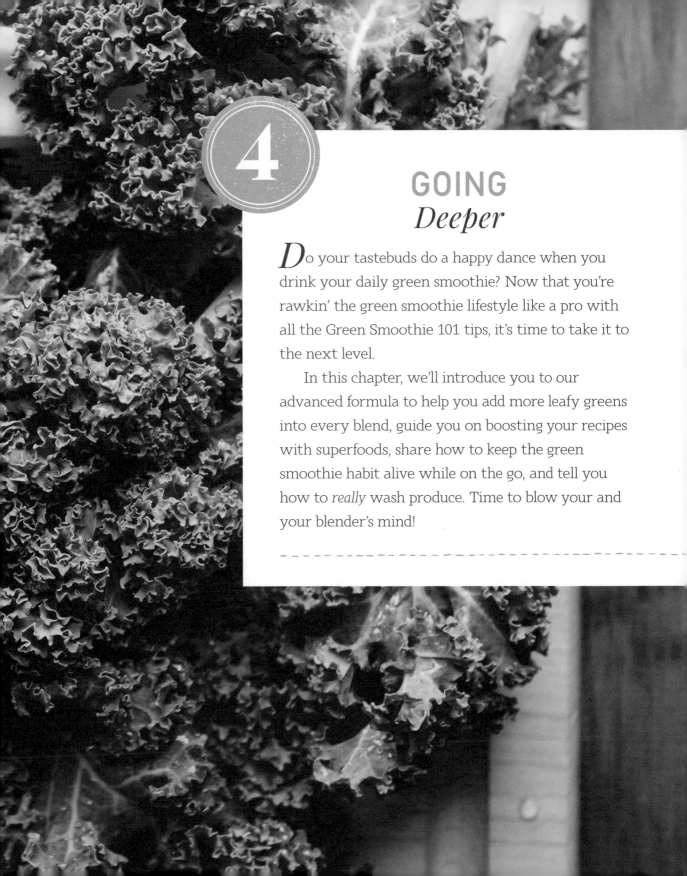

4

GOING
Deeper

*D*o your tastebuds do a happy dance when you drink your daily green smoothie? Now that you're rawkin' the green smoothie lifestyle like a pro with all the Green Smoothie 101 tips, it's time to take it to the next level.

In this chapter, we'll introduce you to our advanced formula to help you add more leafy greens into every blend, guide you on boosting your recipes with superfoods, share how to keep the green smoothie habit alive while on the go, and tell you how to *really* wash produce. Time to blow your and your blender's mind!

FALLING MORE IN LOVE WITH LEAFY GREENS

You've mastered the Rawkstar Recipe Formula with 2 cups of leafy greens and 3 cups of fruit in the 10-Day Kick Start. The cool thing is it's pretty likely that this beginner-friendly ratio we've shared with you might actually start to taste too sweet to you. Crazy, right? First you were freaking out about blending spinach. Now you're a leaf-lovin' rawkstar. Rawk on!

After the 10-day transition, your palate may be ready for the next level of green smoothie making. You may even crave more "hard-core" greens. Start gradually by adding a little more leafy greens to your favorite recipes. Once you work up to about 3 cups of leafy greens and are ready to go further, you can begin cutting back on the fruit. Below are examples of how you can tweak the Rawkstar Recipe Formula as your tastebuds adjust to leafy greens.

Stage I	*Stage II*	*Stage III*	*Stage IV*
2 cups leafy greens	2½ cups leafy greens	3 cups leafy greens	3 cups leafy greens
3 cups fruit	3 cups fruit	3 cups fruit	2 cups fruit
2 cups liquid	2 cups liquid	2 cups liquid	2 cups liquid

GREEN SMOOTHIE BOOSTERS

As you up your green smoothie game, we know you may want to get a little adventurous and boost your green smoothie with even more nutrients. Start with one boosting ingredient at a time; then, once you have tried a few, you can mix and match.

HEADS UP! Anytime you see green smoothie boosting ingredients in a recipe, just know that they're optional and can be skipped at any time (especially if they're expensive or hard to find).

Meal Replacement Green Smoothie Boosters

Green smoothies are a great meal replacement solution. And weight loss is often a happy side effect. If you want to speed up and increase your weight loss results, we suggest you replace a meal each day with a green smoothie. Before you take that first sip, we've got a few rawk-star tips and suggestions to keep you from turning "hangry" until that next meal. (*Hangry* is that feeling of hunger and anger when you've skipped a meal.)

Healthy fats and proteins are the way to go if you want to power up with green smoothies as meal replacements. Healthy fats have amazing superpowers, like protecting your heart, keeping your energy levels up, boosting your metabolism, and lowering bad cholesterol levels. Plant-based proteins help repair your muscles, so these are a must postworkout as well. This combo keeps you feeling full and gives you the energy you need to keep cruisin' until your next meal.

"I lost 27 pounds by having a green smoothie as one meal replacement a day." —JADAH

Here are a few of our favorite combinations of plant-based proteins and healthy fats to add to our green smoothie recipes. Pick one meal replacement booster per two-serving smoothie recipe.

- ¼ cup chia seeds + 2 tablespoons coconut oil
- ¼ cup hemp hearts + ½ avocado
- ¼ cup rolled oats + 2 tablespoons almond butter

- ¼ cup plant-based protein powder + 2 tablespoons coconut oil
- 4 ounces silken tofu + ¼ cup chia seeds
- ¼ cup almond meal + 2 tablespoons coconut oil

Protein Boosters with a Plant-Based Punch

Adding nuts, seeds, and grains to your green smoothies will boost them with an essential macronutrient your body can't live without—protein! This helps prevent blood sugar spikes so you don't feel weak and dizzy. Boost your green smoothies with these protein-rich superfoods.

Chia Seeds

We are obsessed with these tiny, crunchy seeds that make it so easy to boost your green smoothies with protein and healthy fats. Sprinkle chia seeds on top of your smoothie, soak them in water for 10 minutes (to thicken them into a gel-like consistency), or blend them right into your recipe—it's totally up to you!

SERVING SIZE: 2 TBSP | 3 G PROTEIN | FLAVORLESS

Hemp Hearts

Hemp is a complete protein, which means it contains all nine essential amino acids. It can be purchased ground as powder or as shelled hemp seeds, known as hemp hearts. The hemp hearts are more versatile; they can be sprinkled on top of your smoothie, stirred in for a little crunch, or blended whole.

SERVING SIZE: 2 TBSP | 4 G PROTEIN |
LIGHT NUTTY FLAVOR (HEMP HEARTS), EARTHY (HEMP POWDER)

Flaxseeds

Flaxseeds have a stronger flavor than hemp hearts or chia seeds, yet they definitely do the body good. Ground flaxseeds are easier for your body to digest than whole flaxseeds so buy them whole for maximum shelf life, then use a coffee grinder to grind the seeds and get their full nutritional value. (Make sure to use the freshly ground seeds within a week so they don't go rancid.)

SERVING SIZE: 2 TBSP | 4 G PROTEIN | SUBTLE NUTTY FLAVOR

Did You Know?

Drinking a protein-rich smoothie after a work-out is an excellent way to maintain muscle mass and burn fat. When your body has enough protein, it'll choose to burn fat over protein to get the energy it needs. Check out more protein-packed smoothie recipes for before and after your workout in Chapter 9.

Almond Butter

There are many kinds of nut butters to choose from, but our favorite is almond butter. Almonds (along with cashews and hazelnuts) are high in magnesium, which plays a key role in converting sugar to energy. They're filled with fiber to keep your blood sugar levels even, and the protein helps stave off hunger. Look for raw or dry-roasted almonds with no added ingredients. Almond meal (also known as ground almond flour) is great to add to green smoothies, too.

SERVING SIZE: 2 TBSP | 7 G PROTEIN | NUTTY

Oats

Oats are a great plant-based protein that provides magnesium, fiber, and potassium (aka long-lasting energy during your workouts!). Look for old-fashioned (rolled) oats, which haven't been processed like instant oats, because they retain more of their nutritional value and flavor. Oats are superfilling and help stabilize your blood sugar levels, so you don't hit a sugar high and then crash hard. You can add oats to your green smoothies raw, soaked overnight, or slightly heated.

SERVING SIZE: ½ CUP, DRY | 7 G PROTEIN | NUTTY

Quinoa

This mighty little seed happens to be packed with protein and fiber (and is gluten free!). Cooked, quinoa (pronounced "KEEN-wah") adds that filling grain texture that our bodies crave (hello, healthy carbs!). The best part is that quinoa is a complete protein, which means it has all nine of the amino acids that your body needs. Quinoa flakes and flour are available as well and might be easier to blend into your next green smoothie—and they make digesting easier, too.

SERVING SIZE: ½ CUP, COOKED | 4 G PROTEIN | SLIGHTLY NUTTY

Healthy Fat Boosters That Fuel

Add just a couple of tablespoons of healthy fats to your green smoothie to help curb your appetite and give you a quick energy boost. We all can use some more of that, right?

Coconut Oil

So what makes this oil so special? Well, 90 percent of coconut oil is composed of medium-chain fatty acids (or triglycerides), which are easily digested and sent right to the liver for energy production. Because it travels directly to the liver, it is not stored as fat and actually can help boost your metabolism. Look for organic, virgin coconut oil, and buy the good stuff for a little more money.

SERVING SIZE: 1 TBSP | 14 G FAT | MILDLY SWEET AND CREAMY

Avocado

We always have avocados on our counters, and they all seem to ripen at once! We'll add a ripe one to a smoothie and cut the rest to freeze for future green smoothies. An avocado is the creamy green gem of smoothie making and has almost 20 vitamins and minerals that boost heart health and keep your skin soft and glowing. Start with 1 tablespoon and feel free to work your way up to a whole avocado if you like your green smoothies thick and creamy (which we definitely do!).

SERVING SIZE: ¼ CUP | 5 G FAT | VERY MILD TASTE

Flaxseed Oil

Flaxseed oil contains both omega-3 and omega-6 fatty acids, which support healthy brain development (super important for pregnant mamas). Flax is loaded with lignin, a phytonutrient that has antibacterial, antifungal, and antiviral properties.

SERVING SIZE: 1 TBSP | 13 G FAT | SLIGHT NUTTY FLAVOR

TIP: We recommend purchasing flaxseed oil that is sold in black bottles (which are better at blocking out light and so preserve the oil better). Store it in the refrigerator.

Cashews

Adding cashews to green smoothies gives you a dreamy combo of healthy fats and protein. Raw and unsalted cashews are our favorite way to go! Soaking nuts and seeds helps break down any "antinutrients," which interfere with the absorption of nutrients. This helps your body absorb all the beneficial vitamins and minerals. The soaking process is also particularly helpful for those who need to be extra gentle on their tummies because of digestive issues. However, you may notice that your stomach is just fine digesting raw nuts and seeds, and if that's the case, feel free to skip the soaking step in the name of simplicity and efficiency in the kitchen.

SERVING SIZE: 2 TBSP | 12 G FAT | A HINT OF SWEETNESS

TIP: We're having a cashew crush, but feel free to use any nuts, such as almonds, macadamia nuts, pecans, Brazil nuts, or walnuts, in your green smoothies to add a healthy boost of fats.

Soaking Times for Nuts and Seeds

8+ HOURS	4–8 HOURS	2–4 HOURS	DON'T SOAK
Almonds	Brazil nuts	Cashews	Hemp seeds
Flaxseeds	Pecans	Sunflower seeds	Pine nuts
Hazelnuts	Pistachios		
Macadamia nuts	Walnuts		
Pumpkin seeds			
Sesame seeds			

HOW TO SOAK:

1. Add nuts or seeds to a glass bowl, pour in room-temperature filtered water, and cover the bowl with a dish towel (to allow it to breathe) while they soak. Follow a 2:1 ratio (2 parts water to 1 part nuts or seeds; for example, 2 cups water to 1 cup almonds).

2. After the nuts or seeds have soaked for their recommended time, drain the water, rinse, and add them to your recipe. Make sure to rinse until the water appears clear.

PSSST... You can soak nuts for up to 2 days at room temperature (in case you forget about that bowl of nuts on your counter, like we do all the time).

SUPERFOODS PLUS BOOSTERS

Superfoods are known to fuel you with extra energy, so you can rock your workout and bypass that afternoon slump. But we have to let you in on a little secret: Your local fruits and veggies are superfoods, too! They just don't have all that cute packaging (or the price tag).

If you're looking for new ways to add nutritional variety, however, the following five are great ones to start with and will make your green smoothie super-duper nutritious! These are just a few of our favorite ingredients, and we share them as a simple and easy way to start incorporating new superfoods into your green smoothies. But they're not essential; they're optional and can easily be omitted from any recipe. So don't freak out if you can't seem to find these ingredients or if adding them would break the bank.

Cacao

We love cacao (pronounced "ka-cow") for two reasons: It's loaded with antioxidants and it has a chocolate flavor! Antioxidants boost your immune system, which helps your body fight those nasty colds and other sicknesses. To get the benefits of these antioxidants, make sure you're consuming cacao in its raw form, which is spelled *c-a-c-a-o*. You'll want to combine raw cacao with something naturally sweet to bring out the rich chocolate taste in your green smoothies. Cacao powder or nibs taste great with creamy ingredients like bananas, avocado, coconut, nut butters, and nut milks, as well as cherries, strawberries, and raspberries.

SERVING SIZE: 2 TBSP | NOT QUITE AS SWEET AS THE "CHOCOLATE" YOU KNOW

Açaí

Açaí (pronounced "uh-sigh-ee") is a small purple berry found in the rain forests of Brazil and usually consumed as a puree or powder. These tiny berries are known to be loaded with antioxidants that keep your skin healthy and boost your energy and ability to focus. Açaí pairs well with coconut water, spinach, or bananas. It can be found in most local health-food stores and in the frozen-foods aisle as puree smoothie packs. Feel free to swap any recipe using açaí with mixed berries and vice versa.

SERVING SIZE: 3.5 OZ (FROZEN PACKAGE); 1 TSP (POWDER) |
A DISTINCTIVE FLAVOR BETWEEN SWEET AND TART
(LIKE RASPBERRY OR BLACKBERRY)

Goji Berries

Goji berries are loaded with antioxidants, are rich in vitamin A, and have 4 grams of protein per serving; think of them as healing strength packaged in a tiny, sweet berry. With more than 20 vitamins and minerals (including zinc, iron, and beta-carotene), goji berries have been used for centuries in Asian cultures to strengthen eyesight, fight against viruses, balance hormones, and even assist with longevity. For a natural energy boost, sprinkle a few goji berries on top of any of your favorite smoothie bowls.

SERVING SIZE: 1 OZ (ABOUT 3 TBSP) | SEMISWEET AND TANGY

Maca

Maca is known as Peruvian ginseng. It is used as a holistic pain reliever as well as a treatment for other ailments such as anemia, low libido, menopause-related symptoms, and chronic fatigue. If you're looking for a natural mood-and-energy booster, try adding some raw mighty maca powder along with creamy ingredients like bananas and avocado to your next green smoothie.

Taking too much maca may throw your hormones out of whack, so make sure to consult with your health care provider before incorporating this into your green smoothie routine.

SERVING SIZE: ½ TSP | SLIGHTLY SWEET, EARTHY "MALTED"

Spirulina

If you're ready to take your chlorophyll love to the next level, try adding a pinch of spirulina's alkalizing green goodness to the rotation. Spirulina is a plant algae that contains loads of nutrients, the top two being protein and omega-3 fatty acids. Spirulina helps your body release heavy metals and toxins and is high in iron and antioxidants that fight off free radicals, so it's an excellent superfood for those courageous enough to add a pinch or two to their green smoothies. The taste is strong (some even say pond scum–esque), so start small as you work your way up to acquire this supernutritious taste. Once you've added the spirulina to your green smoothie, drink it fresh and fast. You don't want to let it sit too long, since the flavor just gets stronger. If you're not a fan of the taste, two rawesome chlorophyll-loaded alternatives are chlorella and wheatgrass.

SERVING SIZE: ½ TSP (OR UP TO 2 TSP IF YOU'RE REALLY BRAVE) |
STRONG, INTENSE OCEAN FLAVOR

SPICE BOOSTERS

A dash of spice can transform a smoothie into a treat in seconds. Yet the pleasant taste isn't the only benefit of these four superspices—they all pack a powerful healthy punch that keeps us coming back for more.

Ginger

This healing root has a strong bite, so start small. A ¼-inch piece is about 1 teaspoon grated, and a ½-inch piece is about 2 teaspoons grated. Ginger helps with nausea, gas, and inflammation. We recommend using fresh gingerroot for your green smoothies, although ground ginger could work in a pinch.

Ground Red Pepper

Ground red pepper is insanely potent and adds a spicy kick to your green smoothie, so use it sparingly. It also boosts your circulation, revs up your metabolism, and curbs your appetite.

Cinnamon

Cinnamon is a great immunity booster and contains both calcium and iron. Its warming scent is known to have a very energizing effect on the mind.

Turmeric

Known as the King of all Spices for its potential role in natural healing (according to *Prevention* magazine, it might ease arthritis pain and could help prevent Alzheimer's disease), turmeric is a keeper and should be used when you need to ease aches and decrease inflammation.

How to prep, cut, and store fresh ginger

1. Use a spoon to scrape the peel off the entire root.

2. Slice the root into ¼-inch-thick pieces.

3. Lay the ginger on a baking sheet in a single layer and place in the freezer for 1 hour.

4. Transfer the frozen ginger to a freezer-safe container and return to the freezer until ready to use.

FOUR RAWESOME HERBS

Herbs are flavorful, act as a natural filter for your body, and are oh-so-cleansing.. One of our favorite rawkstar tips is to store your herbs in a Mason jar. Fill the jar with fresh water and place on the counter like you would a fresh bouquet of flowers. Just make sure to trim the ends and change the water (at least every other day). This option is great for herbs with longer stems, like cilantro, parsley, and basil.

You'll want to experiment with adding herbs into your green smoothies; it's best to start small with just a sprig or two to find what tastes good to you. Get ready to add an extra nutritional zing to your green smoothie with these four herbs:

Basil

Basil has a warm flavor that will boost your green smoothies and strengthen your kidneys. The kidneys play a major role in removing waste products and toxins from your bloodstream, like those produced from a diet that includes highly processed foods. The best part is that basil is easy to grow at home by either planting it in your garden or purchasing a small basil plant to leave on your kitchen counter.

Cilantro

If you're looking to add a refreshing citrusy flavor to your next green smoothie, try cilantro. This herb is known for a variety of nutrients, but its ability to bind to toxic heavy metals and remove them from our bodies is what makes it a rawkstar in our eyes.

Mint

The mighty mint helps with toxin buildup, which can occur in the stomach and colon when improper digestion takes place. When you're looking for soothing relief from cramping, bloating, or constipation, mint is the herb you want to add to the mix. Our favorite green smoothie recipe with fresh mint and raw cacao powder is the Skinny Mint on page 217—we're pretty sure it's calling your name!

Parsley

Parsley is another herb with a distinctive flavor that can liven up any green smoothie with a fresh and light herbaceous taste. There are three main filters in the body—the bladder, kidneys, and liver—and parsley is here to assist them all in the detoxification process. Parsley specifically targets any buildup in these filters and helps flush it out of the body.

GREEN SMOOTHIES ON THE GO

Here's how we make sure we get a daily green smoothie while we're away from home.

Traveling on a Plane with a Blender

When I travel, I place my Mason jar with lid on inside my blender container. I use a cozy hand-knit sleeve around the Mason jar to protect it from banging inside the blender. Then I place my blender base inside my backpack and angle the blender jar on top. I personally like to take my backpack with blender inside the plane as a carry-on, but I've also bubble-wrapped my blender and stored it in my checked luggage. The TSA can be a little curious about what's in my bag, but it always makes it through security with no problem. Sometimes I think my blender should have its own passport! —Jadah

Road Trippin' with Green Smoothies

I've learned that bringing a cooler, a blender, cups, and straws is just part of the road-trip packing job. We always have our cooler, which we fill with ice to act as a mini fridge. We'll blend our smoothies in the morning in the hotel room and sip them for breakfast on the road. I usually blend extra, pour it into Mason jars, and store in the cooler for an afternoon snack. At night I'll rinse the cups in the hotel sink and blend again the next day. —Jen

When you arrive at your destination, look for a nearby grocery store and buy one ingredient from each category to keep it simple.

- Leafy greens: fresh spinach or kale
- Frozen fruit: mango, peaches, or pineapple
- Fresh fruit: bananas
- Liquid base: filtered water or coconut water

Not Able to Travel with a Blender?

There are times when we just can't fit our blenders in our suitcases. For trips like that, we make sure to scout out a local juice shop either via the Internet or a personal recommendation. Juice shops carry fresh produce and usually have a blender they are happy to use to make a fresh green smoothie. We've also asked our hotel for a "smoothie favor," and some hotel restaurants have been able to rawk a green smoothie just for us! Another option that's saved us a few times is to find a local health-food store and order from their smoothie bar.

HOW TO (REALLY) WASH PRODUCE

"Do I really have to wash my fruit and veggies?" If you're like us, you've struggled with this one. We like quick and easy, and (really) washing produce is definitely an extra step in the whole green smoothie process. But it's one that's superimportant, and we strongly suggest you don't skip it.

How to Wash Leafy Greens

Store your leafy greens in the fridge until you're ready to use them. Then give them a good wash. You can also wash them immediately and store them in the fridge between paper towels in an airtight container. Another option is to freeze them in a freezer-safe resealable plastic bag (yup, you can freeze your leafy greens), but keep in mind that your smoothie won't be as creamy as when you use fresh leafy greens.

1. Place leafy greens in a bowl of water with a splash of white vinegar.
2. Agitate for 30 seconds to loosen dirt and any bugs.
3. Rinse well with water and pat dry with a clean towel.

How to Wash Berries

Delicious berries need a little extra lovin' to prevent mold and mushiness. Be gentle when washing—and we recommend waiting to do this until right before you're ready to eat them.

1. Place your berries in a colander.
2. Spray generously with produce wash.
3. Rinse well with water.

How to Wash Apples

Apples can be the waxiest of the produce bunch, so you definitely want to give them a good scrub down. We don't recommend peeling your apples, because the skin is full of fiber and vitamins that do the body good.

1. Spray generously with produce wash and let sit for 1 to 2 minutes.
2. Scrub well with a kitchen bristle brush (we dedicate one brush just for washing produce).
3. Rinse well with water.

DIY Produce Wash

This simple yet amazing recipe is from Lindsey Johnson (who took all the smoothie shots for this book and also helped create the recipes). She rawks pretty hard.

- 1 tablespoon organic lemon juice
- 10 drops grapefruit seed extract
- 2 tablespoons baking soda
- 1 cup filtered water
- ¾ cup white vinegar

Combine the lemon juice, grapefruit seed extract, baking soda, water, and vinegar in a pitcher and mix well. Pour into a spray bottle.

GETTING DOWN WITH THE DIRTY DOZEN

× ×

The produce section of the grocery store is a beautiful place with all the fresh fruits and vegetables, but it can also be overwhelming. Conventional, organic, GMO, non-GMO. There are so many choices! The Dirty Dozen list is released annually by the Environmental Working Group (EWG). This guide helps you decide how to buy produce based on exposure to pesticides. The "dirty dozen" are the top contaminated vegetables and fruits when purchased conventionally. The Clean Fifteen are the least contaminated produce.

EWG's 2015 Shopper's Guide to Pesticides in Produce

DIRTY DOZEN

It's important to make an effort to buy these organic when possible, since they are highest in pesticide residue.

Apples
Celery
Cherry tomatoes
Cucumbers
Grapes
Nectarines
Peaches
Potatoes
Snap peas
Spinach
Strawberries
Sweet bell peppers

Plus: hot peppers, kale, collard greens

CLEAN FIFTEEN

It's not as important to buy these organic, since they are lowest in pesticide residue.

Asparagus
Avocados
Cabbage
Cantaloupe
Cauliflower
Eggplant
Grapefruit
Kiwifruit
Mangoes
Onions
Papayas
Pineapples
Sweet corn
Sweet peas (frozen)
Sweet potatoes

Source: Environmental Working Group: ewg.org

Part 2

× × × × ×

SIMPLE GREEN SMOOTHIES

Recipes for Life

5
SIMPLE GREEN
Smoothies

"*The* more, the merrier" doesn't always apply to green smoothie recipes. Combining too many flavorful ingredients can create a tastebud war in your mouth. I'm talking to you, "everything but the kitchen sink" smoothie! Honestly, when you strip a green smoothie down to just five ingredients or fewer, it allows the carefully picked ingredients to be the flavorful rawkstars of the recipe. The ingredients are no longer competing with one another but actually complementing each other, which helps you discern what ingredients you really love.

SIMPLE *Colada* SERVES 2

Simple Colada is a refreshing blend—without the hangover! Kiwifruit is the most nutrient-dense fruit, with plenty of vitamin C, which helps prevent wrinkles and promotes skin rejuvenation.

2 cups spinach

2 cups unsweetened coconut milk

2 cups chopped pineapple *

2 kiwifruit, halved *

1. Blend the spinach and coconut milk until smooth.

2. Add the pineapple and kiwifruit and blend again.

TIP: Want a lighter smoothie? Go for coconut water instead of coconut milk and still get the great tropical flavor!

SIMPLE *Pineapple* SERVES 2

Want to know a secret? Pineapple transforms any green smoothie into a super-refreshing treat and also provides amazing health benefits. It has powerful anti-inflammatory properties and boosts digestion.

2 cups spinach

2 cups water

2 cups chopped pineapple *

1 banana *

1. Blend the spinach and water until smooth.

2. Add the pineapple and banana and blend again.

TIP: Have leftover fresh pineapple? Chop it up, lay it on a baking sheet, and freeze. Then store it in freezer-safe containers until you're ready for a perfectly chilled simple smoothie on another day!

* **Use at least one frozen fruit to make a cold green smoothie.**

SIMPLE *Monkey*

SERVES 2

We're not monkeying around when we say this creamy, chocolatey treat is oh-so-delicious! It tastes so good that you kind of wonder how it can be good for you. Bananas are packed with potassium, which is essential for the muscular and skeletal systems (we like happy bones, too!). Almond butter adds a boost of healthy fats to keep you fueled for hours.

2 cups spinach

2 cups unsweetened almond milk

3 bananas *

4 tablespoons cacao powder

2 tablespoons almond butter

1. Blend the spinach and almond milk until smooth.

2. Add the bananas, cacao powder, and almond butter and blend again.

SIMPLE *Cherry*

SERVES 2

This creamy, antioxidant-rich green smoothie will keep your skin looking and feeling young, thanks to the pigment molecule found in cherries, called anthocyanin, which promotes firm skin and keeps connective tissues strong. The best part is that it's becoming easier to find frozen, pitted cherries at your local grocery store, so you can enjoy them all year long!

2 cups spinach

2 cups unsweetened almond milk

2 cups pitted cherries *

1 banana *

1. Blend the spinach and almond milk until smooth.

2. Add the cherries and banana and blend again.

SIMPLE *Citrus*

SERVES 2

Oranges are packed with vitamin C and provide a healthy dose of sweetness. They make up half the liquid base in this recipe. The fiber helps slow down the release of the fruit sugars, keeping your blood sugar stable while you sip on this sweet treat. Yum!

2 cups spinach
1 cup water
3 oranges, peeled
1 banana *

1. Blend the spinach, water, and oranges until smooth.

2. Add the banana and blend again.

TIP: Peel your oranges with a potato peeler, leaving the inner white peel for the most nutrients.

SIMPLE *Melon*

SERVES 2

We love melons, yes we do, we love melons, how about you? Honeydew, which has high levels of potassium and water, is a great hydrator. This one is especially great for those rawkstars who are in need of a banana-free recipe.

2 cups spinach
2 cups unsweetened coconut water
2 cups chopped honeydew
1 cup chopped pineapple *

1. Blend the spinach and coconut water until smooth.

2. Add the honeydew and pineapple and blend again.

SIMPLE *Greens*   SERVES 2

- -

The mildly sweet pear is combined with tart green grapes, giving your tastebuds a little adventure. The best part is that these two fruits are naturally sweet and tasty but also low on the glycemic index. Feel free to keep the skin on the pear for extra fiber, or peel it for a smoother, less gritty green smoothie.

2 cups spinach

1 cup water

2 cups green grapes *

1 ripe pear, halved and cored *

1. Blend the spinach, water, and grapes until smooth.

2. Add the pear and blend again.

TIP: Wash, measure, and freeze grapes to preserve peak ripeness; then you'll have nature's sweet little ice cubes.

SIMPLE *Berry*   SERVES 2

- -

Diets rich in dietary fiber, which berries have plenty of, have been shown to have a number of beneficial effects, including decreased risk of heart disease. Most grocery stores carry frozen berries and fresh oranges year-round, making this smoothie a rawkstar staple. Simple, convenient, and affordable—that's our favorite way to blend!

2 cups spinach

1 cup water

2 oranges, peeled

2 cups mixed berries *

1. Blend the spinach and water until smooth.

2. Add the oranges and berries and blend again.

TIP: Use coconut milk instead of water to make this recipe creamier.

SIMPLE *Mango*

Let's tango while we blend up some mango! This is a perfectly mild smoothie, loaded with amino acids, antioxidants, and potassium. These power-packed nutrients promote healthy hair and nails and antiaging. Just remember: The riper the banana, the sweeter the smoothie.

2 cups spinach
2 cups unsweetened coconut milk
2 cups chopped mango *
1 banana *

1. Blend the spinach and coconut milk until smooth.
2. Add the mango and banana and blend again.

TIP: If you don't want to wrestle a mango for the meat of the fruit, check out the frozen-fruit section for reasonably priced, year-round frozen mango.

SIMPLE *Apricot*

Apricots are one rawkin' fruit that we love dried, jammed, fresh, and blended! They can be hard to find, but they're well worth the search. If you can't locate apricots, swap in peaches or nectarines. This smoothie is packed with vitamin A, which is important for good vision and a healthy immune system.

2 cups spinach
2 cups water
2 cups apricots, halved and pitted
1 cup chopped mango *

1. Blend the spinach and water until smooth.
2. Add the apricots and mango and blend again.

6

ENERGY
Boosting

*N*eed a little extra pep in your step? Hoping to avoid the afternoon slump? Or maybe you just have an epic day ahead of you and need some natural superpowers. We totally get it, and we often use these recipes ourselves for these very reasons. If your current go-to pick-me-up is a cup of coffee, can of soda, or bar of chocolate, we'd love for you to swap it with one of these energy-packed recipes. Let's carpe diem!

Oh, Kale Yeah!

Kale has blown up in popularity over the past few years and for good reason! It has an insanely high nutrient density, including having more iron per calorie than beef (pound for pound). That's what we call plant power! Adding citrus fruits like oranges, lemons, and limes to kale smoothies helps cut the bitterness and brings out the better side of kale. And a little insider rawkstar tip: Use baby kale for a milder green taste.

KALIFORNIA *Sunshine*

SERVES 2

You'll wake up from your California dreamin' in no time with this energizing citrus-and-kale combo. With more than 130 percent of the recommended daily vitamin C found in each orange, you'll raise your energy levels whether you need a morning reboot or an afternoon pick-me-up. And chia seeds are what the Mayan warriors used for endurance, so this is the perfect boost to sustain your energy throughout the day!

2 cups kale, stems removed

1 cup water

2 oranges, peeled

1 cup chopped pineapple ✳

1 cup chopped mango ✳

2 tablespoons chia seeds

1. Blend the kale, water, and oranges until smooth.

2. Add the pineapple, mango, and chia seeds and blend again.

PINEAPPLE *Banana Bliss*

SERVES 2

If happiness could be bottled up in a Mason jar, it would be this recipe. Bananas are loaded with potassium, fiber, and B vitamins. Every banana contains three different kinds of sugar: glucose, fructose, and sucrose. Glucose and fructose are quickly absorbed into the bloodstream, so they'll give you an energy boost fast. Sucrose acts more slowly, so it keeps your blood sugar levels stable and ensures you don't suffer the crash.

2 cups kale, stems removed

2 cups water

2 cups chopped pineapple ✳

1 banana ✳

Juice of ½ lime

2 tablespoons chia seeds

1. Blend the kale and water until smooth.

2. Add the pineapple, banana, lime juice, and chia seeds and blend again.

✳ **Use at least one frozen fruit to make a cold green smoothie.**

MANGO *Ginger Zinger*

The antioxidant-rich green tea adds a subtle boost of caffeine and a high dose of antioxidants. This caffeine is from a natural source (not the kind you find in soft drinks) and is found in smaller amounts than what is in a cup of coffee. So you don't have to worry about getting the jitters unless you drink a ton of it. Go get your zing on!

2 cups Swiss chard (silverbeet), stems removed

1½ cups green tea, brewed and chilled

½ cup water

2 cups chopped mango *

½ cup chopped pineapple *

1 kiwifruit, halved *

1 piece (½") fresh ginger, peeled

1. Blend the Swiss chard, green tea, and water until smooth.

2. Add the mango, pineapple, kiwifruit, and ginger and blend again.

TIP: Simply brew green tea as stated on the package directions, chill in the fridge, and then blend with your other ingredients and you'll have a caffeine-infused green smoothie!

RISE *and Shine*

SERVES 2

Start the day with the all-mighty Swiss chard. We've fallen madly in love with this leafy green. It's packed with magnesium, iron, and vitamins A, B, C, and K, which provide natural energy and keep your energy levels up and running throughout the day. The coconut oil gives you an extra dose of energy, thanks to its medium-chain triglycerides.

2 cups Swiss chard, stems removed

2 cups water

1 cup blueberries *

2 ripe pears, halved, cored, and peeled *

2 tablespoons coconut oil

1. Blend the Swiss chard and water until smooth.

2. Add the blueberries, pears, and coconut oil and blend again.

CITRUS *Maca Recharge*   SERVES 2

We dedicate this smoothie to you for those days when you are dragging. Maca powder is known for boosting energy levels, thanks to its high amount of minerals (calcium, potassium, iron, magnesium, and zinc), up to 20 essential fatty acids, fiber, carbohydrates, protein, and amino acids. Oranges are vitamin C powerhouses that provide a quick burst of energy.

2 cups spinach

1 cup water

2 oranges, peeled

1 cup raspberries ✳

1 banana ✳

2 teaspoons maca powder

1. Blend the spinach and water until smooth.

2. Add the oranges, raspberries, banana, and maca powder and blend again.

TIP: If you can't find maca powder, use ground chia seeds instead.

PEACHY *Kick Start*   SERVES 2

The sweetness of peaches makes this recipe the perfect kick start to an action-packed morning! The dash of ground red pepper helps boost your metabolism and increase blood circulation, while the ginger gets your blood flowing, which will give you a feeling of having more energy.

2 cups Swiss chard, stems removed

2 cups unsweetened coconut water

2 cups sliced peaches ✳

1 green apple, halved and cored

¼ cup chopped avocado ✳

1 piece (½") fresh ginger, peeled

Juice of ½ lime

Dash of ground red pepper (optional)

1. Blend the Swiss chard and coconut water until smooth.

2. Add the peaches, apple, avocado, ginger, lime juice, and ground red pepper (if using) and blend again.

GREEN *Apple Delight*   SERVES 2

- -

This oat-rageous green smoothie is a winner, folks! Did you know that it takes your body longer to digest oats than to digest raw fruits and veggies, which will give you even longer-lasting energy? We're all about the energy, flavor, and easy-to-find ingredients in this green delight!

2 cups spinach
2 cups unsweetened coconut milk
2 green apples, cored
1 banana *
¼ cup rolled oats
⅛ teaspoon ground nutmeg
⅛ teaspoon ground cinnamon

1. Blend the spinach and coconut milk until smooth.

2. Add the apples, banana, oats, nutmeg, and cinnamon and blend again.

TIP: If you're using apples that were grown conventionally or have a wax coating, we suggest peeling them first.

OH *My Grapefruit*   SERVES 2

- -

Perk up your tastebuds with this citrus-packed recipe. Grapefruit packs a powerful antioxidant punch, keeping your body healthy and strong. Vitamin C will give you the perfect energy pick-me-up, and you'll find plenty of it in the grapefruit, orange, and pineapple.

2 cups spinach
1 cup water
1 grapefruit, halved, peeled, and seeded
1 orange, peeled
2 cups chopped pineapple *
2 tablespoons chia seeds

1. Blend the spinach, water, grapefruit, and orange until smooth.

2. Add the pineapple and chia seeds and blend again.

CARAMEL *Cashew Delight*

SERVES 2

Cashews boast a whopping 5 grams of protein per $\frac{1}{4}$ cup, so you're bound to fall in love with adding cashew milk to your next green smoothie. Cashews are full of magnesium, which plays a key role in converting sugar to energy. Feel free to make your own cashew milk (see the recipe on page 245). You can also easily swap cashew milk for another nut milk, if desired.

2 cups spinach

2 cups unsweetened cashew milk

2 ripe pears, halved, cored, and peeled *

3 Medjool dates, pitted and soaked for 20 minutes

$\frac{1}{2}$ cup raw cashews, soaked for 2 to 4 hours

1 teaspoon vanilla extract

1. Blend the spinach and cashew milk until smooth.

2. Add the pears, dates, cashews, and vanilla and blend again.

TIP: If you know you want this smoothie the next day, put the dates and the 2 cups of cashew milk in a cup in the fridge to soak overnight for some extra creaminess!

TANGERINE *Tang*

SERVES 2

Whether you're working in the garden, relaxin' at the beach, or running in the park, this smoothie is perfect for a sun-filled day. It is loaded with energy-boosting fruits and helps heal skin from harsh sun exposure, thanks to the bromelain found in pineapple. You can swap the coconut water for water or almond milk. It will taste just as good here!

2 cups Swiss chard, stems removed

2 cups unsweetened coconut water

2 tangerines, peeled

1 cup chopped pineapple *

1 banana *

1. Blend the Swiss chard and coconut water until smooth.

2. Add the tangerines, pineapple, and banana and blend again.

7

NATURAL
Beauty

*H*ey, good-looking! It's no secret: Eating a diet high in plant-based whole foods promotes glowing skin, stronger nails, and youthful skin. And who doesn't want more of that? The recipes in this chapter are packed with plant-powered beauty foods that will renew, refresh, and rejuvenate you sip after sip.

SPA *Cleanser* SERVES 2

Ready to enjoy one of the most loved healthy fats? Avocado is rich in oh-so-good-for-you monounsaturated fats, powerful antioxidants, and vitamin E, helping regenerate skin cells for more youthful-looking skin. Coconut water is a beauty indulgence that helps hydrate and regenerate your skin from the inside out. Spinach is loaded with lutein, which keeps your eyes healthy and sparkling.

2 cups spinach

2 cups unsweetened coconut water

2 cups chopped pineapple *

1 avocado, halved, pitted, and peeled *

1. Blend the spinach and coconut water until smooth.

2. Add the pineapple and avocado and blend again.

TIP: If you halve this recipe, make sure you keep the avocado pit intact when you put the remainder in the fridge to keep it fresher longer.

GLOWING *Green Healer* SERVES 2

Blend, sip, and nourish your skin! You'll find plenty of vitamin A in spinach (more than 50 percent of the daily recommended amount per cup), which is essential for healthy eyes and skin. Retinoids come from vitamin A and are known to keep your skin smooth and looking young (wrinkles, hold your horses!). And with more than 100 percent of the daily recommend amount of vitamin C per kiwifruit, your skin will be happy and glowing.

2 cups spinach

3 cups chopped honeydew

2 kiwifruit *

1 banana *

Juice of 1 lime

1. Blend the spinach and honeydew until smooth.

2. Add the kiwifruit, banana, and lime juice and blend again.

TIP: There's no need for an added liquid base in this recipe; once you blend your honeydew, it will liquefy and make 2 cups of melon "juice."

* Use at least one frozen fruit to make a cold green smoothie.

COOL *as a Cucumber*

This supercharged cucumber drink will keep you cool and hydrated. The iron, beta-carotene, folate, and vitamin C in spinach help keep hair follicles healthy and scalp oils circulating. With the sweetness of grapes and the tart zing from the fresh-squeezed lemon, this one is a winner for all the cool cucumber fans around town! If you're new to cucumber, you may want to peel the skin first.

2 cups spinach
1 cup chopped honeydew *
1 cup sliced cucumber *
2 cups grapes *
1 tablespoon lemon juice
2 tablespoons chia seeds

1. Blend the spinach, honeydew, and cucumber until smooth.

2. Add the grapes, lemon juice, and chia seeds and blend again.

TIP: There's no need for an added liquid base in this recipe; once you blend the honeydew and cucumber, it will liquefy and make melon and cucumber "juice."

"My skin looks better, my hair is shiny and smooth, my nails are growing like crazy. I feel more energized, and I'm sleeping more at night. It's absolutely incredible!"

—OLIVIA ZAHALKA

KIWI *Berry Glow*   SERVES 2

This glowing green smoothie has a tropical tang plus a hint of mint that helps ease indigestion and flush out toxins through the skin. Kiwifruit is loaded with vitamin C and antioxidants, which keep skin firm, help prevent wrinkles, and are great for healthy bones and teeth. Pssst . . . did you know kiwi skin is completely edible? Yep. Just scrub the skin with a veggie brush to get it nice and clean and toss it into your blender for an extra boost of fiber and nutrition!

$1\frac{1}{2}$ cups spinach
$\frac{1}{2}$ cup fresh mint leaves
2 cups unsweetened coconut water
2 cups blackberries *
2 kiwifruit, halved *

1. Blend the spinach, mint, and coconut water until smooth.

2. Add the blackberries and kiwifruit and blend again.

FOUNTAIN *of Youth*   SERVES 2

Coconut water paired with watermelon could be its own fountain of youth with its natural electrolytes and high water content. And kale is a great source of beta-carotene, vitamin A, and fiber. So forget your under-eye corrective serum and fuel your body with nature's best organic fruits and veggies.

1 cup kale, stems removed
1 cup spinach
2 cups unsweetened coconut water
1 cup chopped watermelon
1 cup chopped mango *
1 cup chopped pineapple *

1. Blend the kale, spinach, and coconut water until smooth.

2. Add the watermelon, mango, and pineapple and blend again.

TROPICAL *Turmeric Cleanser*

SERVES 2

- -

Hello, gorgeous! If you're looking to nourish and protect your skin from sun damage, then this pineapple-and-turmeric blend may be perfect for you. Pineapple has plenty of vitamin C, which plays a pretty big role in supporting the formation of collagen and overall skin texture. Turmeric is a great pain reliever, but it's also known to help reduce redness in the skin caused by inflammation. And if that wasn't enough to make you do a happy dance, by adding kale to your green smoothies, you're also adding a great antioxidant boost.

2 cups kale, stems removed
¼ cup cilantro
2 cups unsweetened coconut water
2 cups chopped pineapple ✳
1 cup chopped mango ✳
Juice of ½ lemon
½ teaspoon ground turmeric

1. Blend the kale, cilantro, and coconut water until smooth.

2. Add the pineapple, mango, lemon juice, and turmeric and blend again.

REFRESH-*Mint*   SERVES 2

- -

This smoothie is a refreshing treat with a cool kick from the sweet aroma of mint. Mint helps activate digestive enzymes, which supports your digestive system. We have to make sure you look good from the inside out! The antioxidants and other phytochemicals found in pineapple and blueberries can protect your skin cells, so there is less chance for skin damage.

1½ cups kale, stems removed
½ cup fresh mint leaves
2 cups unsweetened coconut water
2 cups chopped pineapple ✳
1 cup blueberries ✳
Juice of ½ lemon
2 tablespoons coconut oil

1. Blend the kale, mint, and coconut water until smooth.

2. Add the pineapple, blueberries, lemon juice, and coconut oil and blend again.

PAPAYA *Sunrise*

SERVES 2

Let your hair flow while you sip on this pretty little drink at sunrise on your favorite beach (or at home in your kitchen, dreaming of that dream holiday). With orange and papaya, you'll get an extra dose of vitamin C love, which is great for your skin and your hair. Too little vitamin C in your diet can lead to hair breakage. This green smoothie combo will help boost the blood circulation in your scalp and make your hair follicles extra happy.

2 cups spinach

2 cups unsweetened coconut water

1 orange, peeled

1 cup seeded, peeled, and chopped papaya *

1 cup strawberries *

1. Blend the spinach and coconut water until smooth.

2. Add the orange, papaya, and strawberries and blend again.

TIP: Drink this one quickly because the papaya does congeal and create a different texture.

Papaya Rawkstar Tip

A papaya is ripe once its skin has turned yellow and the papaya gives slightly to palm pressure.

1. Cut off the bottom and top of the papaya with a knife.

2. Slice in half lengthwise and scoop out the seeds and stringy parts with a spoon.

3. Cut each half in half again, so you have four pieces.

4. For each quarter, carefully remove the skin with a paring knife.

5. Cut into chunks.

RADIANT *Cooler*

SERVES 2

Just 1 cup of strawberries has 149 percent of your daily recommended amount of vitamin C, which helps brighten and tighten your skin (hello, forever young!). The watermelon and peaches complement the strawberries, making this the perfect poolside refreshment. Just don't forget your paper umbrella straw!

2 cups spinach

2 cups chopped watermelon *

1 cup sliced peaches *

1 cup strawberries *

1. Blend the spinach and watermelon until smooth.

2. Add the peaches and strawberries and blend again.

TIP: There's no need for an added liquid base in this recipe; once you blend your watermelon, it will liquefy and make melon "juice."

TROPICAL *Beauty*

SERVES 2

We like to add a little bit of coconut oil to our green smoothies because it aids in the absorption of the other nutrients that you are consuming. This smoothie is full of vitamins C and B_6, which boost collagen production and prevent dry skin. Hello, silky, smooth skin!

2 cups spinach

2 cups unsweetened coconut water

1 cup chopped pineapple *

1 cup chopped mango *

2 kiwifruit, halved *

2 tablespoons coconut oil

1. Blend the spinach and coconut water until smooth.

2. Add the pineapple, mango, kiwifruit, and coconut oil and blend again.

PINEAPPLE *Mojito*

SERVES 2

We believe in sharing your beauty secrets. A great way to introduce your friends to your natural beauty regimen is to have a party. Instead of cocktails, whip up a big pitcher of this green smoothie. With the juicy, naturally sweet pineapple, you have a high dose of manganese, which is a mineral that is essential for bone and cartilage formation and healthy skin. Don't forget the squeeze of lime!

2 cups kale, stems removed

¼ cup fresh mint leaves

2 cups unsweetened coconut water

3 cups chopped pineapple ✳

Juice of 1 lime

1. Blend the kale, mint, and coconut water until smooth.

2. Add the pineapple and lime juice and blend again.

Your Natural Inner Glow

One of our favorite ways to enhance our natural beauty is with a daily green smoothie, and here's why. It:

1. HYDRATES. Your skin is your body's largest organ, yet it's the last to take advantage of any hydration you give your body. So drinking plenty of water is really important if you want glowing skin.

2. RENEWS. The antioxidants found in fresh produce help prevent inflamma-tion that causes skin irritation, and the phytochemicals protect against wrinkles. Sounds like a win-win to us!

3. NOURISHES. Fresh fruits, veggies, and leafy greens are loaded with vitamins, minerals, phytonutrients, and antioxidants—all things that promote great skin, hair, and nails.

SOUTHERN *Charm*

SERVES 2

Nothing is more Southern than a smoothie with collard greens! Cantaloupe is known to help with acne and wrinkles (glowing, smooth skin . . . yes, please!). And packed with plenty of vitamin A, the carrots not only help regenerate collagen (your skin's support system) but also have beta-carotene to support your vision, so you can see your beautiful, sun-kissed skin clearly in the mirror!

2 cups collard greens

1 cup water

1 cup chopped cantaloupe

2 cups chopped mango ✳

½ cup chopped carrots

½ cup chopped pineapple ✳

1. Blend the collard greens, water, and cantaloupe until smooth.

2. Add the mango, carrots, and pineapple and blend again.

TIP: The cantaloupe makes up half the liquid base in this recipe; once you blend your cantaloupe, it will liquefy and make melon "juice."

Did You Know?

Glowing skin is linked to proper digestion. The digestive tract is the main way the body dispels toxins, so if it's backed up or out of whack, other organs will step up and help eliminate toxins. The skin is one of these organs, and some side effects of the skin releasing toxins are breakouts, eczema, dullness, and dermatitis.

To keep things moving along, we recommend doing these things every day.

1. Drink a green smoothie.

2. Drink at least 8 cups of water.

3. Move your body enough to sweat.

8

KID-
Friendly

We know how challenging it can be to get your kids to eat their veggies, especially the leafy green ones. Yet it's not mission impossible! Most kids love sweet, cold treats. These dessert-like beverages are a great way to pack in the leafy greens and make you feel like a supermom (or superdad) at the same time. But you don't have to be a parent to opt in to our kid-friendly recipes. These recipes are perfect for anyone you'd like to help make a smooth transition from salad hater to spinach lover.

BERRY *Blastoff!*

SERVES 2

Do you have a future rocket scientist on your hands? Even if you or your kiddos won't be traveling into space anytime soon, this berry blast will be out of this world. It is supercharged with antioxidants and 2 bananas to keep you fuller longer. Berries taste fantastic and brighten up any kid-friendly smoothie. Plus, adding a handful of berries naturally sweetens your green smoothie as well as providing energy, vitamin C, and fiber.

1 cup spinach

2 cups water

1 cup blueberries *

1 cup strawberries *

2 bananas *

1. Blend the spinach and water until smooth.

2. Add the blueberries, strawberries, and bananas and blend again.

---

3 Ways to Make a Li'l Rawkstar

1. MAKE IT TOGETHER. Involve your kids in the entire smoothie-making process, not just the drinking part. Take them to the store to pick out the ingredients, and then have them measure and blend up the ingredients with you right by their side. When they invest time in making their own green smoothies and know all the ingredients going into them, kids are even more excited to taste the end result.

2. ADD A STRAW. Don't underestimate the power of a straw, especially when kids get to pick it out themselves. We

keep an array of paper, metal, and silly straws in the house so the kids can choose how they want to gulp their greens every day. Just make sure you invest in a straw brush to clean those straws out!

3. HOST A SMOOTHIE RACE. Kids love a challenge, and a smoothie race is no exception. It's incredible how fast and happily you can get your children to gulp down those nutrient-packed smoothies when bragging rights are at the finish line.

---

* Use at least one frozen fruit to make a cold green smoothie.

BANANA *Split*   SERVES 2

Want a sweet treat for your kiddos without the artificial ingredients and sugar overload? We did, too! That's why we created our take on this classic treat—so our kids could feel like they are drinking the most rawkin' Banana Split Milkshake on the block! Top with fresh coconut whipped cream and they will never know that it has a handful of fresh fiber and nutrients included!

1 cup spinach
2 cups unsweetened almond milk
2 bananas *
1 cup cherries, pitted *
2 tablespoons cacao powder
2 tablespoons sliced almonds
Homemade Coconut Whipped
    Cream (optional, page 256)

1. Blend the spinach and almond milk until smooth.

2. Add the bananas, cherries, cacao powder, and almonds and blend again. Pour into 2 glasses and top each with a dollop of coconut whipped cream, if using.

BANANA *Mylkshake*   SERVES 2

Did you know that many restaurant milkshakes are made with more than 50 ingredients (many of which we can't pronounce)? When you and your kiddos are looking for that special drink to hit the sweet spot, give this a blend. They'll never know that it is packed with potassium, protein, and spinach. It can be our little secret.

1 cup spinach
2 cups unsweetened almond milk
2 bananas *
1 ripe pear, halved, cored, and
    peeled *
1 tablespoon vanilla extract

1. Blend the spinach and almond milk until smooth.

2. Add the bananas, pear, and vanilla and blend again.

TIP: Peel the pear for a smoother, less gritty green smoothie.

Did You Know?

Baby leafy greens tend to have a milder flavor than their larger buddies. You can find baby spinach, baby kale, and baby bok choy in most grocery stores, and adding these to your green smoothies will help them taste less "green."

PINKY *Pie Punch*

This sweet knockout smoothie is sure to please. This one, two, three punch is packed with potassium, fiber, and protein. Beets are great to add to smoothies for kids because they add a vibrant pink color without overpowering the taste of the sweet fruits. A great smoothie to start the day off right, we pinkie promise!

1 cup spinach

2 cups unsweetened coconut milk

2 clementines, peeled

1 banana *

1 cup strawberries *

2 tablespoons peeled and chopped raw beet

Homemade Coconut Whipped Cream (optional, page 256)

1. Blend the spinach and coconut milk until smooth.

2. Add the clementines, banana, strawberries, and beet and blend again. Pour into 2 glasses and top each with a dollop of coconut whipped cream, if using.

TIP: Digging the beet? Red Velvet (page 214) and Up Beet (page 203) are two other great smoothies that incorporate beets as well.

"I just wanted to thank you for all the great recipes! I even talked my 10-year-old into doing the challenge, and she loves it. She missed out yesterday morning because she went skiing. But as soon as she got home, she asked, 'Can I have my smoothie now?'"

—CAROLINE ROSCHAT

PEACH *Party*

Party like a rawkstar with this peachy green smoothie! Oranges provide the vitamin C, which is a great natural immunity booster. Peaches are packed full of potassium, which helps build muscle. This fresh and light smoothie is perfect during peak peach season for the most perfect party-in-your-mouth smoothie!

1 cup spinach
1 cup water
2 oranges, peeled
2 cups sliced peaches *
1 banana *

1. Blend the spinach, water, and oranges until smooth.

2. Add the peaches and banana and blend again.

THE *Green Goblin*

This smoothie is our hero by making this superfood drink superfun for our little ones. Blend this power-packed vitamin C booster. Pineapple, banana, and oranges add an amazing amount of creaminess and sweetness to this green smoothie and cover up just about any green taste. No matter the time of year, we love incorporating these simple ingredients for a family favorite drink!

1 cup spinach
2 cups water
2 oranges, peeled
1 cup chopped pineapple *
1 banana *

1. Blend the spinach and water until smooth.

2. Add the oranges, pineapple, and banana and blend again.

THE *Happy Monkey* SERVES 2

You will have one happy kiddo after this sweet treat! This might be your first introduction to hazelnut in a green smoothie, but did you know that it's the secret ingredient in the beloved treat Nutella? Cacao is packed with more concentrated amounts of antioxidants than any other food. So enjoy this Nutella-inspired treat without the guilt.

¼ cup hazelnuts, toasted (see tip)
2 cups unsweetened coconut milk
1 cup spinach
2 bananas ✳
2 tablespoons cacao powder
1 teaspoon vanilla extract

1. Blend the hazelnuts and coconut milk together.

2. Add the spinach and blend until smooth.

3. Add the bananas, cacao powder, and vanilla and blend again.

TIP: To toast hazelnuts, remove the hazelnut skin to boost flavor. Toast the hazelnuts in the oven at 350°F (chopped hazelnuts for 5 to 7 minutes; whole nuts for 10 to 20 minutes).

FRUIT *Cocktail* SERVES 2

Next time you're at the store, reach for the real fruit cocktail: fresh grapes, peaches, a pear, cherries, and pineapple. Then make your own additive-free fruit snack! Grapes are a wonderful natural sweetener and pack a healthy punch of antioxidants. Add frozen grapes to give your smoothie a sweet chill.

1 cup spinach
1 cup water
½ cup grapes ✳
½ cup sliced peaches ✳
1 ripe pear, halved, cored, and peeled ✳
½ cup cherries, pitted ✳
½ cup chopped pineapple ✳

1. Blend the spinach, water, and grapes until smooth.

2. Add the peaches, pear, cherries, and pineapple and blend again.

Green Smoothie Ice Pops

*E*arly on, we realized green smoothies make rawesome ice pops. The kids practically beg to make green smoothie pops once the warm summer days come around. Yet ice pops are just one way we've discovered to get kids super excited about eating their spinach. We've specifically created these two green smoothie ice pop recipes so that they would fit in an ice pop mold set without too much wasted. We also paid attention to making these recipes a perfect ratio for the perfect ice pop texture. Licking fingers is welcome!

POPEYE'S *Greensicles* MAKES 6

"I'm strong to the finish, 'cause I eats me Spinach, I'm Popeye the sailor man!" [toot, toot!] We encourage our kiddos to become strong by eating their greens, and blending it into our favorite frozen treats is the easiest way to do that.

1 cup spinach
1 cup unsweetened coconut milk
2 oranges, peeled
1 banana
1 teaspoon vanilla extract

1. Blend the spinach, coconut milk, and oranges until smooth.

2. Add the banana and vanilla and blend again.

3. Pour into 6 molds and freeze for 5 hours, or until completely frozen.

TIP: If making a smoothie instead of an ice pop, use at least one frozen fruit to make it colder.

DIY *Rawkin' Layered Ice Pops*   MAKES 6

- -

Create this party-worthy delight in a few simple steps.

1. Blend ½ cup spinach, ½ cup water, half a banana, 1 cup chopped pineapple, and 1 cup sliced peaches together.

2. Pour the green mixture into a pourable container and set aside.

3. Blend ½ cup spinach, ½ cup water, half a banana, 1 cup raspberries, and 1 cup strawberries together.

4. Pour the red mixture into ice pop molds (one-third full) and freeze until very thick but not completely frozen (1 to 2 hours).

5. Meanwhile, chill the green puree in the fridge.

6. Once semifrozen, remove the pops from the freezer and pour the green puree into the molds.

7. Insert ice pop sticks into the molds to the desired length and put back in the freezer until semifrozen.

8. Once semifrozen, pull out and add the remaining pink layer.

9. Continue freezing for 4 to 5 hours, or until completely firm.

TUTTI-FRUTTI *Pops*   MAKES 6

- -

Baby steps are the key to helping your children develop a taste for greens in their smoothies. This green smoothie pop will excite even the most cautious in your house.

1 cup spinach
1 cup water
1 cup chopped pineapple
1 cup strawberries
1 cup raspberries
1 cup sliced peaches
1 banana

1. Blend the spinach and water until smooth.

2. Add the pineapple, strawberries, raspberries, peaches, and banana and blend again.

3. Pour into 6 ice pop molds and freeze for 5 hours, or until completely frozen.

9

FITNESS
Fuel

*D*rinking a daily green smoothie isn't a diet—it's a lifestyle. It's about finding a healthy, sustainable lifestyle where you take care of your body. In addition to fueling our bodies with green smoothies, we benefit so much from moving our bodies! As in the good, old-fashioned, increase-your-heart-rate and sweat-it-out kind of exercise. It's all about embracing where you are right now. #rawkstarfuel

Preworkout Green Smoothies

*T*he best kinds of preworkout foods are filled with protein, good carbs, and healthy fats. These ingredients help you stock up on energy and keep you full, so your body is sustained throughout your entire workout.

MIGHTY *Matcha Mango*

SERVES 2

When we say mighty, we mean it! Matcha powder is the superform of green tea, and it sure lives up to its name! "Matcha" means powdered tea, so when you add matcha to your green smoothie, you're ingesting the whole leaves, which means you get a stronger dose of nutrients than you'd get from regular steeped green tea. The antioxidant superpowers found in matcha are known to increase your endurance.

2 cups spinach

2 cups unsweetened coconut milk

2 cups chopped mango *

1 banana *

1 teaspoon vanilla extract

1 teaspoon matcha powder

1. Blend the spinach and coconut milk until smooth.

2. Add the mango, banana, vanilla, and matcha powder and blend again.

TIP: Having trouble finding matcha powder? No worries, this smoothie is still tasty without it. If you really want to get your hands on some mighty matcha, Whole Foods, ThriveMarket.com. Amazon.com, and Vitacost.com typically carry it.

* Use at least one frozen fruit to make a cold green smoothie.

SPICED *Apple Core*

This smoothie is a great one to drink before a high-intensity workout. Why? Because apples contain a powerful antioxidant called quercetin. Quercetin's main role in the body is to deliver more oxygen to the lungs. Now that's powerful fuel for your body!

2 cups spinach
2 cups unsweetened almond milk
2 apples, halved and cored
1 banana ✳
1 piece (½") fresh ginger, peeled
½ teaspoon ground cinnamon
2 tablespoons almond butter

1. Blend the spinach and almond milk until smooth.

2. Add the apples, banana, ginger, cinnamon, and almond butter and blend again.

MORNING *Jump Start*

SERVES 2

Are you a morning person who loves to work out first thing? Try adding oats to your next preworkout green smoothie. Oats provide long-lasting energy during your workout. They also help maintain stable blood sugar levels.

2 cups chard, stems removed
1 cup unsweetened almond milk
2 cups chopped nectarines ✳
1 banana
¼ cup rolled oats
2 tablespoons almond butter
Pinch of ground cinnamon

1. Blend the chard and almond milk until smooth.

2. Add the nectarines, banana, oats, almond butter, and cinnamon and blend again.

TIPS: You can use raw, soaked, or cooked rolled oats.

You can swap nectarines for peaches or apricots.

Five Preworkout Ingredients to Fuel You

Before you get your body moving and sweatin', you need to fuel it. Great preworkout green smoothies are stoked up on healthy fats with a moderate amount of carbs and protein.

× ×

BANANAS: Bananas are loaded with carbohydrates that help energize your body and put you in an extra-good mood, which is perfect for a preworkout buzz. Bananas also contain tryptophan, which your body converts to serotonin. Serotonin is a chemical the body creates for a natural mood booster. You can see why we put bananas at the top of our list.

OATS: Oats make this list for one simple fact: They take a long time to digest. This means that they provide long-lasting energy during your workout. Oats also help maintain stable blood sugar levels during your workout, which is always a good thing. You can add dry oats, soaked oats, or even cooked oats to your smoothie. We usually recommend adding 2 tablespoons of dry oats or ¼ cup of cooked oats to any green smoothie recipe.

APPLES: Apples contain a powerful antioxidant called quercetin. Quercetin's main role in the body is to deliver more oxygen to the lungs.

When you get more oxygen to your lungs during a workout, you have greater endurance. This makes it so much easier to get through that hour-long Spin class!

COCONUT OIL: If you're exercising for weight loss, then coconut oil will be an important ingredient for you. The fatty acids in this superfood fight body fat by converting into energy that boosts your metabolism (as opposed to saturated fats that put on body fat). Add coconut oil to your green smoothie before you work out to help fight body fat. We add 2 tablespoons to our green smoothie recipes.

NUT BUTTERS: The best reason to eat nut butter before a workout is because it's loaded with healthy fats and fiber, which keep you feeling full and energetic throughout your entire workout. There are many kinds of nut butters to choose from, but our favorite is almond butter. We add 2 tablespoons to our smoothies all the time—yum!

BERRY *Power Bar*   SERVES 2

Looking for a raw and more filling preworkout snack? Forget that nutritionally empty, sugar-snack protein bar and opt in for our favorite berry smoothie. With tons of filling and nutrient-packed ingredients, this smoothie will have you saying yes to benching that extra weight or going an extra mile on the track.

2 cups spinach

2 cups unsweetened almond milk

1 cup raspberries *

1 cup strawberries *

2 bananas *

¼ cup rolled oats

1 teaspoon vanilla extract

1. Blend the spinach and almond milk until smooth.

2. Add the raspberries, strawberries, bananas, oats, and vanilla and blend again.

TIP: You can use raw, soaked, or cooked rolled oats.

FIT *Fuel*   SERVES 2

When you are hungry before a workout and want a simple, energizing drink, try Fit Fuel. Bananas contain good carbohydrates, which the body quickly and easily converts into energy before and after a workout. Adding coconut oil to your green smoothie before your workout will help you maintain energy throughout your entire routine.

2 cups spinach

1 cup unsweetened coconut water

1 cup water

1 cup chopped pineapple *

1 cup sliced peaches *

1 banana *

2 tablespoons coconut oil

1. Blend the spinach, coconut water, and water until smooth.

2. Add the pineapple, peaches, banana, and coconut oil and blend again.

TIP: Blend coconut oil at room temperature for a smooth blend; there's no need to preheat it.

Postworkout Green Smoothies

*A*fter a nice and sweaty workout, you need to eat foods that will replenish lost nutrients and help your body rebuild your muscles to be even stronger. The average person needs to consume 10 to 20 grams of protein after a workout, plus good carbohydrates, along with liquid to rehydrate. After your next exercise session, consider trying one of the five recipes below, which we've created specifically to help your body recover from a good workout.

BLUE *Steel*   SERVES 2

Let's see your best blue steel face while drinking this green smoothie! We are striking our poses and rawkin' out to this blueberry- and basil-flavored smoothie. Blueberries are chock-full of antioxidants, specifically the kind that help prevent muscle damage from intense workouts. And coconut water is great for replenishing electrolytes lost during a workout. The rawkstar ingredients found in this postworkout recipe combo should help you recover faster.

1½ cups spinach
½ cup fresh basil
2 cups unsweetened coconut water
2 cups chopped mango *
1 cup blueberries *
2 tablespoons chia seeds

1. Blend the spinach, basil, and coconut water until smooth.

2. Add the mango, blueberries, and chia seeds and blend again.

Eight Ingredients to Help You Recover from a Workout

It's essential to fuel your body with the right nutrients before a workout, and it's just as important to eat the right foods after a workout, too. When you push your body hard during exercise, your heart rate goes up, your muscle fibers break down, and you sweat a lot. These eight ingredients will give your postworkout body some extra love.

NUT BUTTER: Getting enough protein after a workout is crucial for proper recovery. Since nut butter is a great source of protein, it's a great addition to your postworkout meal or smoothie.

HEMP HEARTS: Hemp hearts are also an excellent source of protein and fiber, which makes them perfect for an after-workout snack. They're also well known for their role in repairing muscle.

COCONUT WATER: Coconut water is terrific for replenishing electrolytes lost during your workout. It's lower in calories than most sports drinks, which makes it a much better option.

BLUEBERRIES: Blueberries are chock-full of antioxidants, specifically the kind that help prevent exercise-induced muscle damage. This is very good news for you! Eat some blueberries after your workout, and you'll avoid extra muscle pain and help your muscles recover up to three times faster than normal.

PINEAPPLE: Pineapple is another fruit that is loaded with antioxidants that help you recover from your workout quicker and build muscles faster. Add in the bonus of bromelain, an enzyme that helps keep injury inflammation in check, and you can see why we're so sweet on this tasty fruit!

ORANGES: Oranges are a great addition to a postworkout smoothie. Like kiwifruit, oranges have a lot of vitamin C and potassium, which are really important nutrients to replenish after a workout.

BANANAS: Bananas contain good carbohydrates, which the body quickly and easily converts into energy after a workout. By eating a banana after a workout, you help your body recover quickly and rebuild muscle faster.

SWEET POTATOES: Like bananas, sweet potatoes are packed with carbohydrates the body needs to recover from a tough workout. They're also rich in fiber, vitamin E, and potassium—all nutrients that aid in a quick recovery.

KALE-LICIOUS

SERVES 2

"Kale-licious" means blendin' those kale leaves any chance you get. Postworkout is a great time to get some rawkin' kale power into your system! This dark leafy green is good for hair, nails, and bone health, and it provides protein, iron, vitamins, and minerals. Oh, kale yeah, that's what we're talkin' about! Adding that all-important protein, in the form of almond butter here, will get you refueled and recharged for your next workout.

2 cups kale, stems removed

2 cups water

1 cup blueberries *

1 cup chopped pineapple *

1 banana *

2 tablespoons almond butter

1. Blend the kale and water until smooth.

2. Add the blueberries, pineapple, banana, and almond butter and blend again.

SWEET *Relief*

SERVES 2

After that long run, Pilates class, or weight session, who isn't ready for the feeling of satisfaction and relief that comes from completing something so great for your body? Take that energy and continue with something great for your postworkout body! We have combined the protein and fiber in hemp hearts, the sweetness of pineapple, and the nutrients from sweet potato (healthy carbs, fiber, vitamin E, and potassium) that aid in quick recovery to give you a complete postworkout meal. You can leave the skin on your sweet potato for extra fiber.

2 cups spinach

2 cups unsweetened coconut milk

1 orange, peeled

1 cup cooked sweet potato, chilled

1 cup chopped pineapple *

2 tablespoons hemp hearts

1 piece (½") fresh ginger, peeled

Juice of ½ lime

1. Blend the spinach and coconut milk until smooth.

2. Add the orange, sweet potato, pineapple, hemp hearts, ginger, and lime juice and blend again.

TIP: Use at least one frozen fruit to make the smoothie colder.

TRAIL *Mix* SERVES 2

- -

Just finished a marathon or an intense workout? You'll be happy to load up on cherries. Research shows that cherries help with muscle soreness and inflammation. After your big day, kick up your feet and blend our trail mix smoothie for a sweet recovery. Aaaahhh.

2 cups spinach

2 cups unsweetened almond milk

2 cups cherries, pitted *

¼ cup rolled oats

2 tablespoons almond butter

2 tablespoons cacao powder

1. Blend the spinach and almond milk until smooth.

2. Add the cherries, oats, almond butter, and cacao powder and blend again.

TIP: You can use raw, soaked, or cooked rolled oats.

THE *Green Hulk* SERVES 2

- -

We love our favorite type of fast food—green smoothies! When you are done working out and need something to blend quickly, give the Green Hulk a whirl. With almond milk and almond butter, this smoothie helps your muscles recover.

2 cups Swiss chard, stems removed

2 cups unsweetened almond milk

2 bananas *

1 cup sliced peaches *

2 tablespoons almond butter

1 teaspoon vanilla extract

1. Blend the Swiss chard and almond milk until smooth.

2. Add the bananas, peaches, almond butter, and vanilla and blend again.

10

HEALING &
Immunity Boosting

*T*he immune system is the body's incredible defense network against infections, viruses, and bacteria that enter the body. The stronger your immune system is, the less chance you have of getting sick and the faster you can recover. A diet rich in fruits and vegetables containing immune-boosting antioxidants and vitamins will help you achieve a healthy immune system with all-natural, plant-powered ingredients.

BANANA *Spice*

- -

This all-natural superfood smoothie is the ultimate in boosting immunity. Adding just a ½" chunk of fresh ginger to your green smoothies provides amazing health benefits, like reducing inflammation, aiding digestion, and helping the body naturally detoxify. It may also help alleviate pain—from arthritis to menstrual pain and more. It's like an all-natural ibuprofen, immunity booster, and anti-inflammatory.

2 cups spinach

2 cups unsweetened coconut milk

3 bananas *

1 piece (½") fresh ginger, peeled

½ teaspoon ground cinnamon

⅛ teaspoon ground cardamom

1. Blend the spinach and coconut milk until smooth.

2. Add the bananas, ginger, cinnamon, and cardamom and blend again.

TIPS: For a gut-healing superboost, swap 1 cup coconut milk for 1 cup coconut yogurt.

This recipe makes great ice pops!

A little ginger goes a long way, so if you're not used to using fresh ginger, start off small and add more as your tastebuds adjust. If you're feeling the sniffles or a cold coming on, ginger will help kick that cold to the curb just a bit faster.

* Use at least one frozen fruit to make a cold green smoothie.

WATERMELON *Mojito*   SERVES 2

Watermelon and mint are a superhealing combo, and when blended together in a smoothie, they taste indulgent. Watermelon contains lycopene, which is a powerful antioxidant that can protect against degenerative diseases and help cells function better. Mint contains menthol, which is a natural decongestant that helps break up phlegm and mucus. Blend up this treat when you are feeling under the weather or need to clear your sinuses.

2 cups Swiss chard, stems removed

¼ cup fresh mint, stems removed

2 cups chopped watermelon

2 cups chopped mango ✳

Juice of ½ lime

1. Blend the Swiss chard, mint, and watermelon until smooth.

2. Add the mango and lime juice and blend again.

TIP: There's no need for an added liquid base in this recipe; once you blend your watermelon, it will liquefy and make melon "juice."

WATERMELON *Fresca*   SERVES 2

Watermelon Fresca is the perfect green smoothie for when you're feeling stressed. It's packed with celery, which contains chemical compounds that can lower the level of stress hormones in your blood. Combine that rawesome power with ginger's anti-inflammatory and pain-relieving compounds and you've got one rawkin' green smoothie! This recipe is very juicelike, so feel free to pour it over a few ice cubes and sip in style.

1½ cups spinach

1½ cups chopped celery

¼ cup fresh parsley

2 cups chopped watermelon

1 cup chopped pineapple ✳

1 piece (½") fresh ginger, peeled

1. Blend the spinach, celery, parsley, and watermelon until smooth.

2. Add the pineapple and ginger and blend again.

TIPS: There's no need for an added liquid base in either of these recipes; once you blend your watermelon, it will liquefy and make melon "juice."

CITRUS *Cold Recovery*　　SERVES 2

- -

Catch a cold? Try this green smoothie to help nurse yourself back to health! Beets are loaded with antioxidants like vitamin C, which can help boost your immune system. Flaxseed oil contains both omega-3 and omega-6 fatty acids; having a proper balance of these fatty acids is important for brain function and heart health.

2 cups green cabbage

1 cup water

2 oranges, peeled

2 cups chopped pineapple ✳

1/4 cup peeled and cubed raw
　　golden beet

Juice of 1/2 lemon

2 tablespoons flaxseed oil

1. Blend the cabbage, water, and oranges until smooth.

2. Add the pineapple, beet, lemon juice, and flaxseed oil and blend again.

HEALING *Greens*　　SERVES 2

- -

We love the power of broccoli to keep your body healthy! Apples are loaded with fiber and vitamin C to boost your immune system. An apple a day does keep the doctor (and your cold) away!

1 1/2 cups kale, stems removed

1/2 cup broccoli florets ✳

1 cup water

1 large tomato, halved

1 green apple, halved and cored

1/4 cup chopped avocado ✳

Juice of 1 lemon

Dash of ground red pepper

1. Blend the kale, broccoli, and water until smooth.

2. Add the tomato, apple, avocado, lemon juice, and red pepper and blend again.

TIP: This is a room temperature smoothie; if you prefer it chilled, use frozen broccoli or avocado. You can also add 4 ice cubes or set the blended smoothie in the fridge to chill.

CUCUMBER *Lassi*

SERVES 2

Our re-creation of this traditional (fresh and creamy!) lassi drink provides extra healthy bacteria in the gut. Our guts have more than 100 trillion microbial cells that influence human physiology, metabolism, nutrition, and immune function. When you buy the ingredients for this smoothie, go for organic, if available, so you can consume the skin of the cucumber. It's packed with kidney-cleansing properties and vitamin K.

2 cups spinach

¼ cup fresh mint, stems removed

¼ cup cilantro, stems removed

2 cups unsweetened coconut yogurt

1 cucumber, peeled if not organic

Juice of ½ lemon

¼ teaspoon ground cumin

Pinch of sea salt

1. Blend the spinach, mint, cilantro, and yogurt until smooth.

2. Add the cucumber, lemon juice, cumin, and salt and blend again.

TIP: Trouble finding coconut yogurt? Swap for coconut milk (or your favorite yogurt).

SWEET *Turmeric Twister*   SERVES 2

- -

Got tummy troubles? Turmeric may be just the spice you've been looking for! Turmeric is an anti-inflammatory spice known for its medicinal superpowers. This superfood spice helps heal digestive problems and relieves pain and swelling caused by inflammation. Pairing ginger and pineapple, this smoothie will make your tummy feel like it's getting a nice warm hug.

2 cups spinach

2 cups water

3 cups chopped pineapple ✳

Juice of 1 lemon

1/2 teaspoon ground turmeric

1 piece (1/2") fresh ginger, peeled

1. Blend the spinach and water until smooth.

2. Add the pineapple, lemon juice, turmeric, and ginger and blend again.

TIP: Have a fresh turmeric root? Swap in a 1/2" piece in place of the ground turmeric.

PURPLE *Power Healer*   SERVES 2

- -

Boost your health with this healing elixir! Red cabbage (the purple kind) contains anthocyanins, which studies have shown help suppress inflammation. Elderberry extract is a natural cold and flu fighter, which is why it's always in our fridge! It is also called Sambucus and is considered a natural alternative to synthetic cough-and-cold syrups.

2 cups chopped red cabbage

1 cup water

1 orange, peeled

1 cup blackberries ✳

1 banana ✳

1 teaspoon elderberry extract

1. Blend the cabbage, water, and orange until smooth.

2. Add the blackberries, banana, and elderberry extract and blend again.

TIP: Try red cabbage microgreens; studies show that they can have more vitamin C than full-grown cabbage.

VITAMIN *C Fiesta*   SERVES 2

This smoothie will give your body a rawkin' immune boost with more than 842 percent of the daily recommended amount of vitamin C (that's more than 400 percent per serving)! Red bell peppers, oranges, strawberries, and kiwifruit all pack a powerful vitamin C punch, which is just what you need when you're fighting a cold. It's best to power up on the vitamin as soon as you start feeling cold symptoms to recover the fastest.

2 cups kale, stems removed

1 cup unsweetened coconut water

1 orange

½ cup sliced red bell pepper

2 cups strawberries *

1 kiwifruit, halved

1. Blend the kale, coconut water, and orange until smooth.

2. Add the bell pepper, strawberries, and kiwifruit and blend again.

GETTIN' *Figgy with It*   SERVES 2

Are you getting figgy with it? Figs are a sweet fruit with soft flesh and tiny edible seeds. You can eat figs fresh and raw, with or without their peel. With 4 grams of fiber in each tiny fig, they are a great source of soluble fiber, which is helpful when you need to move things along in the digestion department.

2 cups spinach

2 cups unsweetened almond milk

1 cup figs *

1 cup raspberries *

1 banana *

2 tablespoons almond butter

1. Blend the spinach, almond milk, and figs until smooth.

2. Add the raspberries, banana, and almond butter and blend again.

TIP: Blending figs with almond milk and spinach first helps get rid of the seeds.

TROPICAL *Mango-Rita*

SERVES 2

Meet the tastiest, healthiest hangover cure! You'll need to strengthen your immune system if you've been partying a little too long (or drink this instead at your next party!). In just 1 cup of pineapple, you'll find 52 percent of the Recommended Dietary Allowance of vitamin B_6. This vitamin plays a key role in nerve cell communication, red blood cell formation, and antibody combinations that are needed to fight various diseases. Oh, and the coconut water base is great for replenishing lost electrolytes to help you stay hydrated.

2 cups fresh spinach

1 cup unsweetened coconut water

1 orange, peeled

2 cups chopped mango *

1 cup chopped pineapple *

Juice of ½ lime, plus 2 lime slices for garnish

Coarse salt for rim of glasses (optional)

1. Blend the spinach, coconut water, and orange until smooth.

2. Add the mango, pineapple, and lime juice and blend again. If desired, rub the rims of 2 margarita glasses with the squeezed lime, and then dip the rims in coarse salt. Pour the smoothie into the glasses and garnish each with a lime slice.

11

LEAN
& Green

*I*f you're looking for a recipe with a little less sugar or for a more veggie-heavy smoothie blend, Lean & Green is your chapter. We created the recipes in this chapter with more low-glycemic fruits, such as berries, pears, apples, and cucumbers, which will certainly not mask the leafy green goodness as much as our other more tropical-inspired ingredients do. We even have some full-on veggie-based recipes for the veggie lovers. Say hello to broccoli, dandelion greens, and fennel!

Warning to our rawkstar newbies: The recipes in this chapter might taste "too green" to you. Please take caution when sipping these lean, green smoothie machines.

LEAN *Green Cleanser*

SERVES 2

Lean, green fighting machine! Cucumber has a high water content and actually cools the body down, making this recipe cleansing and hydrating.

2 cups kale, stems removed

1 cup peeled and chopped
   cucumber

1 cup water

1 orange, peeled

1 ripe pear, halved and core *

1 whole lime, peeled

1. Blend the kale, cucumber, and water until smooth.

2. Add the orange, pear, and lime and blend again.

TIP: Want less of a lime taste? Use just the juice of 1 lime.

PEACH *Pear Refresher*

SERVES 2

We've used two low-glycemic fruits, peaches and pears, in this refreshing smoothie to make your tastebuds happy and to keep your blood sugar stable.

2 cups Swiss chard, stems
   removed

2 cups unsweetened coconut
   water

2 cups sliced peaches *

1 ripe pear, halved and cored *

1. Blend the Swiss chard and coconut water until smooth.

2. Add the peaches and pear and blend again.

TIP: Add a squeeze of lemon to brighten the peach and pear flavors.

* Use at least one frozen fruit to make a cold green smoothie.

GINGER *Berry Mojito*   SERVES 2

Ginger is an essential in our personal weekly grocery list. We love adding that extra kick of ginger to spice up our smoothies. And with the ginger-and-mint combo, you have 2 ingredients that are known to help your liver remove toxin buildup naturally. Zing!

2 cups spinach
1/2 cup mint
2 cups unsweetened coconut
    water
2 cups strawberries *
Juice of 1/2 lemon
1 piece (1/4") fresh ginger, peeled
2 tablespoons chia seeds

1. Blend the spinach, mint, and coconut water until smooth.

2. Add the strawberries, lemon juice, ginger, and chia seeds and blend again.

FLORIDA *Fennel Refresher*   SERVES 2

Once upon a time, I met a girl in Florida who loved fennel so much that she would carry it around with her as a snack, no joke! Being influenced by her, I am a converted fennel lover, too. This crisp, licorice-flavored herb has been known to help with digestion, remedying gas, indigestion, and bloating. That's one rawkin' ingredient to fuel our bodies on a hot Florida day!

1 cup water
1 fennel bulb, halved and cored
2 cups spinach
2 oranges, peeled
1 green apple, halved and cored
Juice of 1/2 lemon

1. Blend the water and fennel until smooth.

2. Blend in the spinach and oranges.

3. Add the apple and lemon juice and blend again.

4. Pour over ice to make the smoothie colder.

TIP: Cut the core out of the center of the fennel bulb and add extra blending time for the bulb's tough fibers.

Detox Friendly

*W*e use the term *detox* lightly because the body (especially the rawkstar liver) naturally flushes out toxins daily. That's why we love drinking green smoothies—it's an easy way to help flush out toxins, so the body can use its natural ability to heal itself. There are a few ingredients known to help your body's own detoxification system work more efficiently. Once your body gets a little detox support and love from these ingredients, your liver, colon, and kidneys are happy to work efficiently and effectively, making you feel like a whole new person.

UP *Beet*　　SERVES 2

We love the powerful detox support beets offer our bodies! Beetroot has long been used for medicinal purposes, primarily for disorders of the liver because it helps stimulate the organ's detoxification processes. Beets get a bit of a bad rap because everyone assumes they taste like dirt, and honestly, sometimes they do. We've got you covered so you can enjoy beets and all their nutrients. Simply peel the beets first if you want to add them in raw to remove some of that earthy, gritty taste. If you want to sweeten your beets, roast or steam them (they become even easier to peel once they're cooked). We hope after this recipe, you become up-beet about beets!

2 cups spinach
¼ cup peeled and chopped beet
2 cups unsweetened coconut water
1 orange, peeled
1 cup chopped pineapple
1 cup cherries, pitted ✱

1. Blend the spinach, beet, and coconut water until smooth.

2. Add the orange, pineapple, and cherries and blend again.

AGUA *Fresca Detox*

SERVES 2

All kinds of rawesomeness are packed inside this drink! Leafy greens and basil are good sources of vitamin K, which is used by your body to help blood coagulate, which prevents excess bleeding when a blood vessel is injured. Vitamin K is also essential in forming various proteins necessary for bone formation and repair. Blend these leafy greens together with frozen pineapple and peaches and you'll naturally cool down on those "hot as kale" days!

2 cups spinach
¼ cup basil
2 cups unsweetened coconut water
2 cups sliced peaches ✱
½ cup chopped pineapple ✱
Juice of ½ lime

1. Blend the spinach, basil, and coconut water until smooth.

2. Add the peaches, pineapple, and lime juice and blend again.

DETOXSTAR

SERVES 2

Parsley is great for supporting your body in pushing out the toxins! There are three main filters in the body—the bladder, kidneys, and liver—and parsley is here to assist them all in the detoxification process. Plus, you get a plant-based protein boost with the hemp hearts and a sweet metabolism boost with the cinnamon.

2 cups spinach
¼ cup parsley
2 cups water
2 cups strawberries ✱
1 cup sliced peaches ✱
1 piece (¼") fresh ginger, peeled
2 tablespoons hemp hearts
1 teaspoon ground cinnamon

1. Blend the spinach, parsley, and water until smooth.

2. Add the strawberries, peaches, ginger, hemp hearts, and cinnamon and blend again.

MINT *Julep Sweet Tea*

No bourbon necessary when blendin' this traditional springtime drink! Add the chilled green tea for an antioxidant-filled liquid base, and sweeten this smoothie with peaches and apples! Don't forget to put your pinkie finger out while you drink this tea-infused smoothie. Cheers to your health, darling!

2 cups spinach
¼ cup mint
2 cups green tea, brewed and
    chilled
2 cups sliced peaches ✱
1 green apple, halved and cored
Juice of ½ lemon

1. Blend the spinach, mint, and green tea until smooth.

2. Add the peaches, apple, and lemon juice and blend again.

Low Glycemic

If you need to pay attention to your blood sugar levels, look for fruits that fall below 55 on the glycemic index, such as apples, all kinds of berries, cherries, grapes, pears, kiwifruit, plums, and peaches. Lemons, limes, and oranges are also considered low-GI fruits.

FIELD *of Greens*   SERVES 2

- -

In the Field of Greens, you can dream up any recipe possible! It's where all your leafy green dreams come true. Here, we combine some of our favorite fruits and veggies to make a smoothie that is a home run. Broccoli adds a "green" taste and different texture when blended in your smoothie. This high-fiber veggie keeps your liver healthy and aids in digestion, so we think it knocks it out of the park!

1 cup spinach

1 cup broccoli florets ✱

2 cups unsweetened coconut water

1 orange, peeled

1 cup blueberries ✱

1 apple, halved and cored

1. Blend the spinach, broccoli, and coconut water until smooth.

2. Add the orange, blueberries, and apple and blend again.

COOL *Greens*   SERVES 2

- -

Rawkstar, are you looking for a detox-friendly drink that is supercharged with leafy green goodness? If so, this is your drink! This green smoothie is a vitamin-and-mineral powerhouse. Check out these ingredients: kale, vitamin K; dandelion greens, calcium; cilantro, potassium; water, hydration; celery, vitamin K; pears, fiber; ginger, anti-inflammatory properties; lemon, vitamin C. Your body will thank you later!

1 cup kale, stems removed

1 cup dandelion greens

¼ cup cilantro, stems removed

2 cups water

1 celery rib

2 ripe pears, halved and cored ✱

1 piece (½") fresh ginger, peeled

Juice of 1 lemon

1. Blend the kale, dandelion greens, cilantro, and water until smooth.

2. Add the celery, pears, ginger, and lemon juice and blend again.

VEGGIE-*Licious*   SERVES 2

- -

Drink your veggies! Not only is this recipe low-glycemic, but it's also savory. Adding tomatoes, carrot, and garlic to your blender can encourage you to step out of the norm and explore the world of veggie love.

2 cups spinach

1 cup water

2 cups chopped tomatoes

1 carrot

1/4 cup chopped avocado

1 clove garlic

Juice of 1/2 lemon

1 tablespoon fresh oregano

Dash of salt

1. Blend the spinach, water, and tomatoes until smooth.

2. Add the carrot, avocado, garlic, lemon juice, oregano, and salt and blend again.

TIP: Serve at room temperature or heat up on a cold day for a warm veggie soup!

VEGGIE *Cocktail*   SERVES 2

- -

Love our mocktail version of a Bloody Mary. It's perfect served at room temperature in a Mason jar (with an extra celery stick for garnish). If you're feeling adventurous, add your favorite hot sauce to take it up a notch!

2 cups kale, stems removed

3 cups chopped tomatoes

1 celery rib

2 scallions, sliced

1/4 teaspoon minced garlic

Juice of 1 lime

1/8 teaspoon ground red pepper

Pinch of salt

1. Blend the kale and tomatoes until smooth.

2. Add the celery, scallions, garlic, lime juice, red pepper, and salt and blend again.

12

DELICIOUS
Desserts

*I*f you're anything like us, you may find yourself in
the frozen-foods aisle picking up your smoothie ingredients, and then all of a sudden you're engaged in an
internal debate over the ice cream sale. That's why
we've created the green smoothie recipes in this chapter for the dessert lover in all of us. This chapter is
a real treat! Literally. These incredibly delicious,
dessert-inspired green smoothies will satisfy your
sweet tooth without any of the guilt.

RED *Velvet*

- -

Cacao (unsweetened raw cacao) is the perfect ingredient to add to green smoothies when chocolate cravings hit, but we love it for more than just its taste. Cacao is high in phenols, which means this smooth and rich superfood helps prevent the clogging of arteries in your body. Bottom line? Cacao keeps your heart beating strong. Blend this recipe for you and a loved one!

2 cups spinach

2 cups unsweetened coconut milk

2 cups strawberries ✳

4 dates, pitted

¼ cup peeled and chopped raw or cooked beet

1 tablespoon cacao powder

½ teaspoon vanilla extract (optional)

Homemade Coconut Whipped Cream (optional, page 256)

1. Blend the spinach and coconut milk until smooth.

2. Add the strawberries, dates, beet, cacao powder, and vanilla (if using) and blend again. Pour into 2 glasses and top with coconut whipped cream, if using.

✳ Use at least one frozen fruit to make a cold green smoothie.

SKINNY *Mint*

SERVES 2

On my honor, I was a Girl Scout! But as I got older, I realized I'd rather have the real chocolate-mint flavor of cacao and fresh mint year-round, without the guilt. It's really a win-win. When the Girl Scout cookie cravings hit, reach for this smoothie instead.

1½ cups spinach
½ cup mint leaves
2 cups unsweetened almond milk
2 bananas *
¼ cup chopped avocado *
4 Medjool dates, pitted
2 tablespoons cacao powder
Cacao nibs, for garnish (optional)

1. Blend the spinach, mint, and almond milk until smooth.

2. Add the bananas, avocado, dates, and cacao powder and blend until smooth. Pour into 2 glasses and garnish with cacao nibs, if using.

CINNAMON *Roll*

SERVES 2

Take your grandma's homemade cinnamon roll recipe, add some love and leafy greens, and you have our rawkin' recipe, sure to rawk your grandpa's socks off! And to make this green smoothie extra thick and creamy, use at least ½ cup of full-fat coconut milk (not the light kind). After one sip, you'll feel as if you're enjoying a cinnamon roll directly out of the oven, but without the added sugar!

4 Medjool dates, pitted
2 cups unsweetened coconut milk
2 cups spinach
1 banana *
2 tablespoons almond butter
1 teaspoon ground cinnamon

1. In a medium bowl, soak the dates in the coconut milk for 20 minutes.

2. Blend the spinach and coconut milk mixture until smooth.

3. Add the banana, almond butter, and cinnamon and blend again.

FIGGY *Pudding*

SERVES 2

Now bring us some figgy pudding and a cup of good cheer! We're bringin' the Figgy Pudding straight to you with our green smoothie take on this oh-so-sweet dessert! This recipe is one you'll want to blend each time you find fresh figs at your local store. Figs have a proteolytic enzyme that is considered to be a digestive aid—dessert with nutritional benefits!

1 cup spinach

2 cups unsweetened coconut milk

2 cups figs *

1 banana *

1 teaspoon ground cinnamon

1 teaspoon vanilla extract

1. Blend the spinach and coconut milk until smooth.

2. Add the figs, banana, cinnamon, and vanilla and blend again.

BLUE *Lavender Ice Cream*

SERVES 2

Oh, my lavender—your tastebuds are in for a real treat! Get ready to delight your senses. Floral lavender is a unique ingredient that is potent and delicious. With the mixture of frozen blueberries, dates, and cashew milk, this creamy green smoothie tastes like a dream. A little lavender goes a long way, so 1 teaspoon is all you need! Pssst . . . if you really want to blow your mind, use an ice cream maker.

4 Medjool dates, pitted and soaked for 20 minutes

1½ cups unsweetened cashew milk

2 cups spinach

½ cup cashews, soaked and rinsed

2 cups blueberries ✳

1 teaspoon organic lavender buds (see tip)

1 teaspoon vanilla extract

2 teaspoons lemon juice

1. In a medium bowl, soak the dates in the cashew milk for 20 minutes.

2. Blend the spinach and cashew milk mixture until smooth.

3. Add the cashews, blueberries, lavender, vanilla, and lemon juice and blend again.

TIP: Where to buy lavender buds? They can be found at local health-food stores or through online retailers like Amazon.com or MountainRoseHerbs.com. Look for organic buds to avoid chemicals and pesticides.

MEXICAN *Hot Chocolate*   SERVES 2

We love taking classic drinks and re-creating them with our own healthy flair. We crave a good Mexican Hot Chocolate when it's chilly outside, so it was inevitable that we'd have to find a way to throw handfuls of leafy greens in it! Serve this warm or chilled; either way, you will be pleasantly surprised when you drink this recipe without even noticing the leafy greens, which are packed with antioxidants and protein. Win-win!

1 cup spinach

1 cup unsweetened almond milk, warmed

1 banana

1 tablespoon almond butter

1 tablespoon cacao powder

1/2 teaspoon ground cinnamon

Pinch of nutmeg

Pinch of ground red pepper

Pinch of salt

1. Blend the spinach and warm almond milk until smooth.

2. Add the banana, almond butter, cacao powder, cinnamon, nutmeg, red pepper, and salt and blend again.

THANKSGIVING *in Your Mouth*

SERVES 2

When you're looking for a festive drink, turn to this recipe! Sweet potatoes are high in complex carbs, their natural sugars release slowly into the bloodstream. Make sure to blend the sweet potato skin because it's loaded with fiber, which will give you a healthy, clean sweep.

2 cups spinach

2 cups unsweetened almond milk

1/4 cup water

1 cup sweet potato, baked and chilled

2 cups chopped mango *

1 teaspoon ground cinnamon

1 teaspoon ground nutmeg

1. Blend the spinach and almond milk until smooth.

2. Add the water, sweet potato, mango, cinnamon, and nutmeg and blend again.

PUMPKIN *Pecan Pie*

SERVES 2

Next time you're at the pumpkin patch in autumn, pick up an extra pumpkin to blend. That's right, we love adding pumpkin to smoothies because it's known for being an anti-inflammatory food. Hello, healthy joints, organs, and soft tissues! Add a little bit of almond milk and a couple of bananas and you have an undeniably "sweet as pie" smoothie.

4 Medjool dates, pitted and soaked

1 cup unsweetened almond milk

2 cups spinach

1 cup water

1/2 cup canned or fresh pumpkin, chilled (see tip)

2 bananas *

1/2 cup pecans, soaked and rinsed

1. In a medium bowl, soak the dates in the almond milk for 20 minutes.

2. Blend the spinach and almond milk mixture until smooth.

3. Add the water, pumpkin, bananas, and pecans and blend again.

TIP: If you're using fresh pumpkin, bake it at 375°F for about 1½ hours for a medium sugar pumpkin, or until tender. Chill in the fridge overnight before blending.

TOASTED *Coconut Almond Fudge*

SERVES 2

- -

Blend this recipe up for a new take on fudge! Truly there are no words to describe this extra sweet treat (and we mean sweet!). If you have a serious sweet tooth (like us), then sip to your heart's content to curb your cravings.

4 Medjool dates, pitted

2 cups unsweetened coconut milk

¼ cup shredded coconut

2 cups spinach

2 ripe pears, halved, cored, and peeled *

3 tablespoons cacao powder

2 tablespoons almond butter

1. Soak the dates in the coconut milk for 20 minutes.

2. Preheat the oven to 350°F. Bake the coconut for 5 minutes, or until lightly browned.

3. Blend the spinach, dates, and coconut milk until smooth.

4. Add the pears, cacao powder, and almond butter and blend again.

5. Pour into 2 glasses. Sprinkle the coconut on top.

PEACH *Pie*   SERVES 2

- -

This subtly sweet treat is the perfect combo of fiber-rich peaches and metabolism-boosting cinnamon! Cinnamon adds a hint of sweetness without the added sugar. The rich coconut milk is a great source of iron and manganese, but if you want to lighten up this smoothie, you can swap in almond milk instead.

2 cups spinach

2 cups unsweetened coconut milk

3 cups sliced peaches *

½ teaspoon ground cinnamon

1 teaspoon vanilla extract

1. Blend the spinach and coconut milk until smooth.

2. Add the peaches, cinnamon, and vanilla and blend again.

TIP: To make this smoothie creamier and sweeter, add a frozen banana.

13

SMOOTHIE
Bowls

*I*t's time to swap your straw for a spoon—it's smoothie bowl time! You can shake up your green smoothie routine and turn your favorite fruits and leafy greens into a thick and creamy smoothie bowl. Simply decrease the amounts of liquids and use frozen fruits and you're good to go. And make sure to use as many frozen fruits as possible to create the perfect smoothie bowl texture. One of our favorite things about a smoothie bowl is all the fun toppings you can pile on it—fresh fruit, nuts, granola, chia seeds, cacao nibs, you name it! *Bon appétit!*

Green Smoothie Bowl Formula   SERVES 2

Any green smoothie recipe can be transformed into a thick and creamy smoothie bowl. You'll just need to cut back on the liquid base to create the proper thickness and use all frozen fruits to give it an extra chill factor.

× ×

1–2 cups leafy greens
1 cup liquid base
3 cups frozen fruit (frozen fruit = extra creamy and cold)

1. Blend the leafy greens and liquid base together.

2. Add the fruit and blend again. Use a long spoon or a tamper to push down the ingredients in between blending. Depending on your blender, you may need to pause and push down the frozen fruit with a spoon and blend multiple times to get the desired consistency.

3. Divide the mixture between 2 bowls. If desired, jazz it up with fresh fruit and crunchy toppings. And for a crazy sweet topping, drizzle a little maple syrup or honey over the top.

RED *Hot Love*   SERVES 2

We love adding a little healing spice to smoothies with the balanced sweetness of berries. Cinnamon slows the rate at which the stomach empties after meals, reducing the rise in blood sugar levels after eating, and the red pepper speeds up your metabolism. The two spices together make a harmonious blend that's sweet and spicy!

1 cup spinach
1 cup unsweetened coconut milk
1 large banana *
1 cup strawberries *
1 cup raspberries *
½ teaspoon ground cinnamon
¼ teaspoon ground red pepper

1. Blend the spinach and coconut milk until smooth.

2. Add the banana, strawberries, raspberries, cinnamon, and red pepper and blend again.

CREAMY *Banana*   SERVES 2

If you're a banana lover like us, you have to try this one! This bright green smoothie bowl is a winner, plus you know by now that we love to fuel our bodies with the best antioxidants in town. Matcha powder is optional, but it's great for energy and endurance. Adding a little lemon will kick this recipe up a notch with the vitamin C.

2 cups spinach
1 cup unsweetened coconut milk
4 large bananas *
2 avocados, halved, pitted, and peeled *
2 tablespoons fresh lemon juice
½ teaspoon matcha powder (optional)

1. Blend the spinach and coconut milk until smooth.

2. Add the bananas, avocados, lemon juice, and matcha powder (if using) and blend again.

TIP: Top with hemp hearts, shredded coconut, granola, fresh berries, or sliced kiwifruit.

* **Use at least one frozen fruit to make a cold green smoothie.**

AÇAÍ *Smoothie Bowl* SERVES 2

This traditional smoothie bowl is the perfect recipe to start with. Açaí (pronounced *"ah-sah-EE"*) is similar in flavor to a grape and a blueberry, but it contains less sugar, with just 2 grams per 4 ounces of berries. This thick and creamy treat is delicious topped with granola for that perfect breakfast or as a treat anytime of the day.

1 cup spinach
1 cup unsweetened almond milk
2 cups mixed berries *
2 packages (3.5 ounces each) unsweetened açaí puree
1 large banana *

1. Blend the spinach and almond milk until smooth.

2. Add the berries, açaí puree, and banana and blend again.

TIP: Top with granola, fresh fruit, nuts, and seeds.

HAPPY *Melon* SERVES 2

If you're happy and you know it, blend this smoothie bowl! With its combination of leafy greens, watermelon, sweet strawberries, and fresh herbs, this smoothie bowl is the perfect snack when you need a mood-boosting pick-me-up. This is a more airy smoothie; if you'd like a thicker texture, add a frozen banana. There's no need for an added liquid base in this recipe—once you blend your watermelon, it will liquefy and make melon "juice."

1 cup spinach
3 cups chopped watermelon, chilled
2 cups strawberries *
2 tablespoons chopped fresh basil

1. Blend the spinach and watermelon until smooth.

2. Add the strawberries and basil and blend again.

TIP: Top with fresh basil, chopped watermelon, and chopped strawberries.

DREAMY *Avocado*

SERVES 2

You'll love this Dreamy Avocado bowl with its savory and creamy souplike texture. This is one of those recipes that you'll be hesitant to try, but you'll be surprised and delighted once you taste how refreshing it is, especially if you top it with cilantro.

2 cups spinach

3 cups chopped cucumber

1 cup chopped avocado
(1 medium)

1 cup chopped celery

½ cup cilantro, including stems

2 tablespoons fresh lime juice

½ teaspoon minced garlic

Pinch of sea salt

1. Blend the spinach and cucumber until smooth.

2. Add the avocado, celery, cilantro, lime juice, garlic, and salt and blend again.

TIP: Serve this smoothie bowl at room temperature and top with chopped celery, sliced cucumber, chopped avocado, extra cilantro, and red chili flakes.

AUTUMN *Bliss*

SERVES 2

When autumn rolls around, the pumpkin-flavored items hit the stores. Enjoy this rendition of all things pumpkin with a seasonal smoothie bowl that's sure to delight your tastebuds.

1 cup spinach

1 cup unsweetened almond milk

1 cup cooked pumpkin puree,
chilled

2 bananas ✳

1 cup frozen cranberries ✳

1 teaspoon pumpkin pie spice

1. Blend the spinach and almond milk until smooth.

2. Add the pumpkin puree, bananas, cranberries, and pumpkin pie spice and blend again.

TIP: Top with dried cranberries, granola, pomegranate seeds, and pecans.

GAZPACHO

- -

Looking for a smoothie bowl with a veggie twist? If so, this is your answer! Gazpacho is a cold soup made entirely of raw vegetables. And, of course, we had to add 2 cups of leafy greens—in this case, romaine, which is packed with vitamins A and K. These 2 vitamins are great for bone health. Next time you have friends over, serve this healthy bowl with some sunflower seeds on top and enjoy this rawfully rawkin' recipe!

2 cups chopped romaine

½ cup cilantro, stems removed

2 cups chopped tomatoes
　　(2 medium)

2 cups peeled and chopped
　　cucumber

½ cup sliced red bell pepper

Juice of 1 lemon

Pinch of sea salt

1. Blend the romaine, cilantro, and tomatoes until smooth.

2. Add the cucumber, bell pepper, lemon juice, and salt and blend until smooth.

TIP: Serve at room temperature and top with chopped cucumber, tomatoes, cilantro, and avocado, plus a lemon wedge and a drizzle of olive oil.

CARROT *Cake*

SERVES 2

Carrot Cake always sounds healthy, but it's usually loaded with a lot of sugar. (After all, it's cake!) Though nothing can truly replace your favorite carrot cake recipe, we are happy to share a healthy take on this classic dessert. Feel free to roast your raw carrots for a smoother, stronger taste. And if you don't mind a nutty texture, you can top your smoothie with a few chopped walnuts, which will add protein, not to mention ample doses of heart-healthy potassium and energy-boosting magnesium.

1 cup chopped romaine

1 cup unsweetened coconut milk

2 cups chopped raw carrots

1 cup chopped pineapple *

1 large banana *

2 clementines, peeled

½ teaspoon vanilla extract

Dash of ground cinnamon (optional)

Dash of ground nutmeg (optional)

1. Blend the romaine and coconut milk until smooth.

2. Add the carrots, pineapple, banana, clementines, vanilla, cinnamon (if using), and nutmeg (if using) and blend again.

TIP: Top with fresh Homemade Coconut Whipped Cream (page 256), toasted shredded coconut, walnuts, chopped fresh pineapple, or a little extra sprinkle of cinnamon and nutmeg.

RAINBOW *Love*   SERVES 2

Taste the real rainbow! Even the pickiest of picky smoothie drinkers will fall in love with this vitamin C–packed recipe. This deep purple smoothie bowl (thanks to the blueberries) will be loved by all ages.

2 cups spinach
2 oranges, peeled
1 cup strawberries *
1 cup blueberries *
1 large banana *

1. Blend the spinach and oranges until smooth.

2. Add the strawberries, blueberries, and banana and blend again.

TIP: Use fresh strawberries, blueberries, and oranges for a textured, colorful topping. We also like to top with freshly sliced kiwifruit.

CHERRY *Quinoa Bowl*   SERVES 2

This low-GI smoothie bowl is different from any other smoothie we've created. We're adding quinoa, a superfood packed with 24 grams of protein and 12 grams of fiber per 1 cup (but we recommend you start with ¼ cup per serving until you adjust to the taste). We've combined with our favorite sweet and high-antioxidant fruit, cherries, for one rawkin' smoothie bowl!

1 cup Swiss chard, stems removed
1 cup unsweetened almond milk
3 cups cherries, pitted *
½ cup cooked quinoa
1 teaspoon vanilla extract
½ teaspoon ground cinnamon

1. Blend the Swiss chard and almond milk until smooth.

2. Add the cherries, quinoa, vanilla, and cinnamon and blend again.

TIP: Top with nuts and seeds, chia seeds, and grated lemon peel.

14

DIY
Recipes

Store-bought nut milk is now more convenient and a great alternative to dairy milk. Yet not all nut milks are created equally, so it's important to read the labels and try to avoid any added sugars such as carrageenan. If you want complete control over the ingredients, the freshness, and the thickness of your milk, you can make your very own nut milks. It's a little more time and labor intensive, but we think making your very own smooth and silky nut milk creation is worth the wait!

HOMEMADE *Almond Milk*

MAKES 4 CUPS

- -

For a long time, we avoided making our own almond milk. We thought it was a complicated process that wouldn't be worth it. Wow, were we wrong. Homemade almond milk is a hundred times better than store-bought! And once you soak your nuts, it takes only 15 minutes to make the whole thing. Plus, it's way more flavorful and super creamy.

1 cup raw almonds (or other raw nuts)
3 cups water
Pinch of sea salt
1 teaspoon vanilla extract
Juice of ½ lemon (optional)
2 tablespoons pure maple syrup (optional)
Pinch of cinnamon (optional)

1. In a bowl, cover the almonds in 2" of water and the lemon juice (if using) and soak at room temperature for at least 8 hours.

2. Drain and rinse the almonds well.

3. Place the almonds and water in the blender.

4. Blend at high speed until smooth (about 2 minutes).

5. Strain and squeeze the mixture through a nut milk bag or cheesecloth into a bowl.

6. Stir in the salt, vanilla, maple syrup, and cinnamon (if using).

7. Transfer to an airtight container and refrigerate immediately.

TIP: Nut milk is best consumed within 3 days. As it sits, it will separate. Simply shake the container and the milk will be creamy again.

rawstar tip - - - - - - - - - - - - - - - - -

For cashew milk, follow the same directions,
except soak the cashews for 4 hours.

HOMEMADE *Coconut Milk*

Ready to taste the best coconut milk ever? It can be difficult to find coconut milk that is free of additives, stabilizers, and gums. (We're looking at you, carrageenan!) Making it at home is as easy as can be: All it takes is 3 ingredients and a few simple kitchen tools, and 15 minutes later, you'll have creamy, rich coconut milk.

3 cups water
1 cup dried unsweetened coconut
Pinch of sea salt

1. In a medium saucepan, bring the water to a boil. Remove from the heat, add the coconut and salt, and soak for 10 to 15 minutes.

2. Pour the coconut mixture into the blender and blend on high speed for 2 minutes.

3. Place a strainer over a bowl and set a nut milk bag inside (or line with cheesecloth).

4. Pour the mixture through the nut milk bag and squeeze out as much liquid as you can.

5. Transfer the liquid to an airtight container and refrigerate immediately.

TIP: Coconut milk is best consumed within 3 days. As it sits, it will separate (the thick top layer is actually coconut cream). Simply shake the container and the milk will be creamy again.

Delicious Nut-Free Milks

*T*here are some delicious nut-free alternatives that you can whip up in your blender! When making any recipe that calls for nut milk, you can substitute with nut-free milk such as oat, rice, hemp, or coconut. You may find yourself doing a little happy dance down your health-food store aisle because many of these stores now carry these nut-free milks. We like easy and we like convenience, but there's nothing more empowering than making your own yummy creation from scratch.

HOMEMADE *Nut-Free Milk*   MAKES 5 CUPS

1 cup hemp hearts, steel-cut oats*, or cooked brown rice
3 cups water
1 tablespoon coconut oil (optional)
2 tablespoons maple syrup (optional)
$\frac{1}{2}$ teaspoon vanilla extract (optional)
Pinch of sea salt

1. Place the hemp hearts (or soaked steel-cut oats, or cooked brown rice) and water in a high-speed blender.

2. Blend on high speed for about 2 minutes, or until fully liquefied.

3. Strain through a nut milk bag or cheesecloth into a wide glass bowl.

4. Discard the pulp from the bag.

5. Rinse the blender and pour the milk back into the blender from the bowl.

6. Add the coconut oil, maple syrup, vanilla (if using), and salt. Blend for 10 seconds.

* Soak steel-cut oats in a covered bowl of water for 20 minutes prior to blending.

JEN'S *Coconut Granola*

2 cups old-fashioned rolled oats
¼ cup almond meal
¾ cup sliced almonds
¾ cup shredded unsweetened coconut
1 teaspoon ground cinnamon
¼ teaspoon salt
5 tablespoons coconut oil
½ cup pure maple syrup
1 teaspoon vanilla extract

1. Preheat the oven to 300°F. Line a baking sheet or pizza pan with parchment paper. (The best way for me is using a pizza pan with airholes in it. I put the parchment paper on that, and the granola comes out nice and crisp.)

2. In a large bowl, combine the oats, almond meal, sliced almonds, coconut, cinnamon, and salt.

3. In a small saucepan, heat the coconut oil and maple syrup. Add the vanilla and whisk to combine. Pour over the oat mixture and stir until well coated.

4. Spread the granola mixture on the baking sheet in a thin, even layer. Bake for 30 minutes, stirring every 10 minutes, or until the granola is golden brown. Let cool completely.

5. Store in an airtight container for up to 1 month.

HOMEMADE *Almond Nut Butter*

Depending on where you live, almond butter can be insanely expensive. Yet there's a cost-effective solution that tastes even better than store-bought. Enjoy!

2 cups raw almonds, roasted if desired (see tip)
2 tablespoons unrefined coconut oil, melted
1 teaspoon sea salt

1. Place the almonds and oil in a high-speed blender or food processor.

2. Slowly speed up the blender to maximum speed, pushing down the mixture as it creeps up the sides of the blender.

3. Continue to blend until the nuts transform into a warm, creamy paste. This can take between 1 and 25 minutes, depending on your equipment and whether you roast the almonds first. Add the salt and blend to combine. Because of the potentially lengthy blending time, perseverance may be part of the process. Yet eventually you'll have some of the creamiest, yummiest nut butter in the world.

TIP: To speed up the process, you can lightly roast the almonds first. This releases their oils for faster blending. Roast at 350°F for 10 to 15 minutes. Not a fan of almonds? You can substitute with Brazil nuts, cashews, hazelnuts, or macadamia nuts.

rawkstar tip - - - - - - -

Want creamier nut butter? Instead of 2 cups of almonds, follow the exact directions above, but use 1 cup raw almonds and 1 cup raw cashews.

"I make homemade vanilla extract because as a baker and a foodie, I like the highest-quality ingredients, as well as the knowledge of exactly what is in what I bake, eat, and drink. My favorite way to make this recipe is to use recycled jars (for a homey touch) and share the finished product with as many friends as possible, because how can something so good not be shared?" —ERIN MOTTAYAW

HOMEMADE *Vanilla Extract*

Did you know that store-bought vanilla extract often contains additives like corn syrup, which is a highly processed sugar? When I realized this, I reached out to my friend Erin, who also happens to be an amazing baker, and she told me that true vanilla extract has only 2 ingredients: vanilla beans and alcohol. When making your own, you get to skip the additives and focus only on the good stuff. This is Erin's go-to recipe, which she kindly shared with Jadah and me. We really like the flavor and sweetness we get when we use Madagascar vanilla beans and a midrange bourbon, such as Kentucky Gentleman. You can also use whiskey, which gives it a darker, bolder flavor and is less sweet.

2 cups bourbon (at least 80 proof; you want it good and strong)
4 Madagascar vanilla beans

1. Pour the bourbon into a pint-size airtight container (a Mason jar works great).

2. Cut an incision along each vanilla bean and open the beans wide.

3. Completely submerge the beans in the bourbon and seal the container.

4. Store in a dark, cool place and shake the mixture weekly.

5. After 60 days, enjoy your very own vanilla extract. (Once the vanilla beans aren't submerged anymore, remove them from the jar.)

TIPS: Store for up to 1 year. As you use up the vanilla extract, you can replenish it with more bourbon and vanilla beans. Just make sure the beans are completely submerged in the bourbon to prevent mold.

When using homemade vanilla extract in recipes, use half the amount called for because it is stronger than most store-bought versions.

HOMEMADE *Coconut Whipped Cream*

- -

Decadent plant-powered whipped cream is possible and delicious. Bonus: It takes only a few minutes to make. Bon appétit!

$\frac{1}{2}$ cup coconut cream
2 teaspoons maple syrup
1 teaspoon vanilla extract

1. Place a mixing bowl and whisk in the freezer for 5 minutes to chill.

2. Pour the coconut cream into the chilled bowl and whip until light and fluffy (peaks will form).

3. Add the maple syrup and vanilla and whip again.

A Coconut Milk Trick

Having trouble finding coconut cream? Have no fear! You can use a can of full-fat coconut milk instead, but it takes a little extra work.

1. Refrigerate the can of coconut milk overnight.

2. Flip the can upside down and open it.

3. Pour out the coconut milk (the liquid). You should have about $\frac{1}{2}$ cup of thick cream left in the can.

4. Scoop out the cream and whip as directed above.

Share Your Rawkstar Story

• •

Your green smoothie journey and inner transforma-
tions are all sunshine in our in-box! You can share in
any one of the following ways. Leafy green hugs
coming your way!

1. ONLINE: Fill out our form at
http://sgs.to/share.

2. FACEBOOK: Post your story and pics to our
Facebook wall or tag us on your own wall with
@simplegreensmoothies.

3. INSTAGRAM: Hashtag us in your IG post,
#simplegreensmoothies.

Join the Movement

*T*ogether, we're creating a healthier, happier world. When we put our health first, we have more energy available for the people we love. When we fill our bodies with the good "green" stuff, we also fuel our passions. When we take care of ourselves, we can take better care of our world.

The Simple Green Smoothies lifestyle started as a personal passion of our own and has grown into a movement that's changing the world—one green smoothie at a time. And you, my friend, are a part of that!

You've embraced one simple habit, and now we invite you to join our rawkstar community. We're a global green smoothie lovin' tribe, and we can't wait to welcome you with open arms and kale kisses! We believe that drinking one green smoothie a day is just the beginning of your journey to health. We invite you to continue this habit and join our next live (and free!) 30-Day Green Smoothie Challenge at sgs.to/30day. Thank you for letting us be in your corner; we truly appreciate the opportunity to cheer you on, no matter where you are on your path.

Peace, love, and leafy greens,

Jen and Jadah

x x x x x x x x x x x x x x x x x x x x x x x x x x x x x

For more recipe inspiration, tips, and resources on how to add more fruits and veggies into your life, join our green smoothie lovin' tribe at SimpleGreenSmoothies.com.

Rawesome Resources

RAWKSTAR CONVERSION GUIDE

LEAFY GREENS

1 cup = 30 grams = 1 ounce

2 cups = 60 grams = 2 ounces

LIQUIDS

½ cup = 125 milliliters

1 cup = 250 milliliters

1½ cups = 375 milliliters

2 cups = 500 milliliters

FRUITS

1 cup = 250 milliliters

1½ cups = 375 milliliters

2 cups = 500 milliliters

SPICES, PROTEINS, AND SUPERFOODS

½ teaspoon = 2 milliliters

1 teaspoon = 5 milliliters

2 teaspoons = 10 milliliters

1 tablespoon = ½ fluid ounce = 15 milliliters

2 tablespoons = 1 fluid ounce = 30 milliliters

RAWKSTAR NUTRIENT AND VITAMIN GUIDE

This guide highlights which fruits and veggies to add to your green smoothies to up your daily dose of essential vitamins, minerals, and nutrients.

Minerals and Nutrients

Calcium

Essential for healthy bones and teeth. It is also needed for normal functioning of muscles, nerves, and some glands.

- Almonds
- Bok choy
- Collard greens
- Kale
- Oranges
- Spinach
- Turnip greens

Fiber

Diets rich in dietary fiber have been shown to have a number of beneficial effects, including decreased risk of coronary heart disease, improved blood sugar control, and better weight management.

- Apples
- Apricots
- Avocados
- Blackberries
- Broccoli
- Cherries
- Coconut
- Mangoes
- Nectarines
- Oatmeal
- Pears
- Raspberries
- Spinach
- Starfruit
- Strawberries

Iron

Helps boost energy levels and is needed for healthy blood and normal functioning of all cells.

- Almonds
- Coconut flakes
- Coconut milk
- Coconut water
- Raspberries
- Spinach

Magnesium

Magnesium is necessary for healthy bones and is involved with more than 300 enzymes in your body! Inadequate levels may result in muscle cramps and high blood pressure.

- Almonds
- Avocados
- Bananas
- Cashews
- Coconut water
- Kale
- Spinach
- Swiss chard
- Walnuts

Manganese

Essential for bone and cartilage formation and healthy skin.

- Avocados
- Bananas
- Beets
- Blackberries
- Blueberries
- Coconut water
- Honeydew melon
- Kale
- Kiwifruit
- Papaya
- Peaches
- Peas
- Pineapple
- Pumpkin
- Raspberries
- Romaine
- Spinach
- Strawberries
- Sweet potatoes
- Tomatoes

Potassium

Potassium is essential for the muscular and skeletal systems—its primary functions are to build muscle and control the electrical activity of the heart.

- Apricots
- Avocados
- Bananas
- Broccoli
- Cantaloupe
- Cherries
- Coconut flakes
- Coconut milk
- Dates
- Kale
- Kiwifruit
- Nectarines
- Peaches
- Spinach
- Sweet potatoes

Vitamins

Vitamin A

Keeps eyes and skin healthy, helps promote bone growth, keeps the immune system strong, fights disease as a powerful antioxidant, and maintains a vigorous reproductive system.

- Apricots
- Cabbage
- Cantaloupe
- Carrots
- Collard greens
- Grapefruit
- Kale
- Mangoes
- Papaya
- Peas
- Pumpkin
- Romaine
- Spinach
- Sweet potatoes
- Tomatoes
- Watermelon

Vitamin B$_6$

Vitamin B$_6$ is responsible for causing chemical reactions that are essential for many tasks throughout the body, including the production of amino acids, neurotransmitters, hemoglobin, and nucleic acids responsible for genetic information.

- Almonds
- Avocados
- Bananas
- Broccoli
- Sweet potatoes

Vitamin B$_9$ (folate)

Healthful diets with adequate folate may reduce a woman's risk of having a child with a brain or spinal cord defect.

- Avocados
- Beets
- Broccoli
- Collard greens
- Kale
- Mangoes
- Oranges
- Romaine
- Spinach
- Turnip greens

Vitamin C

Vitamin C helps the body heal from cuts and wounds. It also increases the amount of iron your body absorbs from foods. Thanks to its ability to keep your immune system healthy, vitamin C is a powerful ally if you're trying to avoid or kick a cold or other illness.

- Apricots
- Avocados
- Bananas
- Blackberries
- Blueberries
- Broccoli
- Cabbage
- Cantaloupe
- Clementines
- Collard greens
- Grapefruit
- Grapes
- Honeydew melon
- Kale
- Kiwifruit
- Lemons
- Limes
- Mangoes
- Melon
- Oranges
- Papaya
- Peaches
- Pears
- Peas
- Pineapple
- Plums
- Raspberries
- Red peppers
- Spinach
- Squash
- Starfruit
- Strawberries
- Sweet potatoes
- Tomatoes
- Watermelon

Vitamin E

Vitamin E is a powerful antioxidant that helps protect cells from damage. Think: healthy, youthful-looking skin. It also plays a role in preventing a range of diseases and maintaining a healthy immune system.

- Almond butter
- Almonds
- Avocados
- Blueberries
- Hazelnuts
- Mangoes
- Red peppers
- Spinach
- Swiss chard
- Tomatoes
- Turnip greens

Vitamin K

Vitamin K makes proteins that cause blood to clot when you're bleeding. It is also essential in forming various bone proteins necessary for bone formation and repair.

- Avocados
- Beet greens
- Blackberries
- Blueberries
- Broccoli
- Cabbage
- Carrots
- Celery
- Collard greens
- Grapes
- Kale
- Peas
- Romaine
- Spinach
- Turnip greens

RAWKSTAR SUBSTITUTION GUIDE

Get ready for some smoothie-savvy swaps! Allergies and inaccessibility to ingredients can definitely make you shy away from certain green smoothie recipes. Yet have no fear! We've compiled a list of great substitutions so you can still reap the rawesome results.

INGREDIENT	SWAP WITH . . .
Almonds, raw	Any other raw nut: Brazil nuts, cashews, hazelnuts, walnuts
Apples	Another variety of apple, pears
Apricots	Peaches, nectarines, mango
Bananas	Avocados (for same creamy texture)
Beets	Carrots, red cabbage
Blackberries	Blueberries, raspberries, cherries, strawberries
Blueberries	Blackberries, raspberries, cherries, strawberries
Broccoli	Cauliflower, cabbage
Cabbage	Spinach, bok choy, romaine, chard, watercress
Cantaloupe	Honeydew or another melon variety, peaches, papaya
Carrots	Sweet potatoes, beets, pumpkin
Cashews, raw	Any other raw nut
Cherries	Blackberries, raspberries, blueberries
Cilantro	Parsley, basil
Coconut water	Filtered water
Collard greens	Kale, beet greens, spinach, Swiss chard, bok choy
Cranberries	Cherries, raspberries, pomegranate arils
Fennel	Celery (for texture) and anise seeds (for flavor)
Garlic	Shallot
Ginger, fresh	1 tablespoon fresh ginger = ½ tablespoon dried ground ginger
Grapefruit	Clementine, orange, tangerine

INGREDIENT	SWAP WITH . . .
Honeydew	Cantaloupe or another melon variety, green grapes
Kale	Arugula, watercress, spinach, Swiss chard, green cabbage, collard greens, beet greens
Kiwifruit	Mango, orange, tangerine, lime
Lemon	Lime, orange, tangerine, clementine
Lime	Lemon, orange, tangerine, clementine
Mangoes	Peaches, nectarines, papaya, apricots
Nectarines	Peaches, mangoes, apricots
Oranges	Clementines, tangerines, mangoes, papaya
Parsley	Kale, arugula, watercress
Peaches	Nectarines, mango, apricots
Pears	Apples, peaches, nectarines, plums
Pineapple	Oranges, mangoes
Plums	Apricots, peaches, nectarines
Pomegranate arils	Cranberries, pineapple, strawberries
Raspberries	Blackberries, blueberries, cherries, strawberries
Romaine	Spinach, Swiss chard, beet greens
Strawberries	Blueberries, raspberries, cherries, blackberries, peaches, nectarines
Swiss chard (silverbeet)	Kale, spinach, romaine, collard greens, beet greens, cabbage, watercress, arugula
Tangerines	Oranges, clementines
Watermelon	Cantaloupe, honeydew

RAWKSTAR SUPPLIES

Here's a list of places where we personally shop for green smoothie supplies. These are not the only places that carry smoothie supplies but the ones that work best for us and that we enjoy supporting. Happy shopping!

Fresh Produce

Trader Joe's

Whole Foods

Costco

Local grocery store

Farmers' markets: To find local farmers' markets, farms, and CSAs, check out localharvest.org.

Superfoods

Rawkstar Shop: sgs.to/essentials

Amazon: Amazon.com

Vitacost: Vitacost.com

Thrive Market: ThriveMarket.com

Blenders

Vitamix: sgs.to/Vitamix-deals

Blendtec: sgs.to/Blendtec-deals

Other rawkstar-approved blenders: Amazon.com

Straws, Lids, and Mason Jars

Mason Bar Company: TheMasonBarCompany.com

Amazon: Amazon.com

Acknowledgments

*O*ur journey as authors would not be possible without our rawkstar community. Thank you for sharing the green smoothie lifestyle with people you love. We love you!

We couldn't have written this book without the amazing support from our SGS Rawkstar Family. Dan Mottayaw, aka the Boss, Lindsey Johnson, you continue to blow our minds. Jessie Provience, thank you for caring so much about our community and for all your hustle and recipe testing! (P.S. Happy birthday, Rowan!) Shauna Bryant, Trish Dubes, Amanda Frisbie, and Jenny Solar, thank you for supporting us with your gifts to help SGS when we needed you most.

We'd also like to thank Scott Hoffman and Steve Troha, who are rawkstar literary agents. There are no other people we'd rather run around New York City with in the rain than you two. We're deeply appreciative to our rawkstar editor, Marisa, and Team Rodale for believing in our message and helping us turn it into the book of our dreams.

A big thank you to our Rawkstar Recipe Testers: Tatjana Pasalic, April H. Machan, Martina Romano Pistarini, Marieve Wilson, Debra Techlin, Meghan Williams, Kelsi Wilson, Janny Organically, Kathi O'Neill, Holly Twist, Lois Weidenbach, Maureen Gibson, Alicia Martinez, Rachael Telford, Neil Madden, Anjanette Hook, Nancy Mann, Jen van Vlymen, Amanda Pentilae, Beth Mastroianni, Lois Battle, Krystle Jordan, Christine Stierly, Melissa Bethel, Cynthia Wright, Trisha Thorme, Tina Oostdyke, Dustin Landfried, Cheryl Bolan, Katie Jaynes, Sharmayne Burns, Anita Smith, Lauren Shaber, Takeia Fields, Tara Huffman, Cheryl Bolan, Mary Yoder, Katie McQuaid, Jeremy and Debby Seerveld, Sonal Gupta, Luis Roman, Janis McGuffin, Stephanie Groman, Donnisha Jones, Jennifer Quint, Claudine Dassoy, Meghan Langley, Julia Landis, Jeni Thompson, Kristina Veenker, Nicole Kinniry, Rachel Templin, Amy Groome, Kimberly Bergman, Jeannie Wilcox, Keith Hurt, Amy Crocker, Rebecca Schmidt, America Brown, Gaoxue Stoppel, Jessica Baluyot, Joy Jonah, Erin Mottayaw, Chris Ettinger, Erica Peterson, Tess Farmer, Jenni Cannariato, Martha Cothron, Hannah Jehring, Katie Jaynes, Nicole Mazzei-Williams, Samuel Mitchell Hughes, Lynn Bourque, Trevor Hanson, Renee Larsen, Max Grant, Peggy Chaffee, Dale Mullings, Meghan Churchill, Barbara Ford Wilson, Korey Hester, Joy Spears, Aimee Dewar, Nicole Hughes, Roy and Anita Herrington, Carly Wellhausen, Isabelle Estrella, Sharon Rice, Carrie Eischens, Heather Merrett, Brian Weber, Alexis Munroe, Krissy Velasco, D. Brown, Tara Will, and Toni Boyd.

From Jen:

This book is a culmination of the love, support, and prayers of my family and friends. I will be forever in awe of how it came to be and am so grateful to you all. To my love of 17 years, Ryan—marrying you was the *best* decision of my life. You've always believed in me and loved all of me. My heart is yours forever. Jackson and Clare, the stars shone brighter the day God brought you both into my life. Thanks for your patience and enthusiasm surrounding this book— your hugs, kisses, and green smoothies were exactly what I needed.

Mom and Dad, from dance recitals, cross-country races, and home renovations to editing this manuscript, you have been there. You have *always* been there. You fill me with love and give me the confidence to dream big. Every page of this book has a piece of you in it. Special thanks to my big sister, Stephanie, for being the human guinea pig on some delicious . . . and some truly nasty green smoothie recipes. You took a few for the team, and I love you even more for that. To my little brother, Mike (who isn't so little anymore)—your support means so much to me. Sweeney, thank you for always believing in me—your love texts always come when I need them most.

To Kaley Moore, Erin Mottayaw, and Lori Benefiel—thanks for pulling me out of the dark literary hole for chats, family dinner parties, cross-country phone calls, and encouraging texts. Thanks to Pastor Jerry and Calene Pence for always being just a phone call away. You've encouraged us and helped our family when we needed it most. It's an honor to serve with you. Jadah—thanks for sharing that first green smoothie recipe with me. I'm blessed and honored to be on this wild adventure with you.

From Jadah:

George Brian, my love, my humble rawkstar, my lovie. After 12 years, you're still my favorite. I love you more and more every day. Thank you for dreaming with me and making sure I laugh often and see the sun. Zoe, you bring me so much joy as I watch you grow. I love being your mama. Thank you for all of the green smoothie races and dance parties.

Mommy, thank you for believing in me and letting me fall, fail, and flourish. Seriously, I feel like I won the daughter lottery because I have you as a mom. And Big Mike, thank you for taking such good care of my mom—you are a great teacher. To my father, Darrell, who taught me to chase my dreams and do what I love no matter what. To all of my family, I love each and every one of you. Special sibling shout-outs to Jamila, Isaiah, Max, and Trinity. God has blessed me with an amazing tribe.

A big thank-you to Auntie Tutti for not only seeing my potential and nurturing the entrepreneur in me but also for making me my very first green smoothie. You are the origi-

nal green smoothie rawkstar. My Nguyen, eternal gratitude to you for pushing me to share green smoothie recipes on Instagram and, of course, for the late-night coffee-shop work dates. Thank you, Michelle Long, for your grace and grit. Brainstorming and dreaming with you is the best. And to my partner in kale, Jen. Love making our dreams a reality together. #heart&hustle

Index

Underscored page references indicate boxed text. **Boldface** references indicate photographs.

A

Açaí, **92**, 93
   Açaí Smoothie Bowl smoothie, 232, **233**
Accessories, 23–24
Agua Fresca Detox smoothie, 204, **205**
Allergies, 6, 40
Almond butter, 87
Animal-based products, 6
Appetite, curbing. *See* Cravings
Apples
   Field of Greens smoothie, **208**, 209
   Florida Fennel Refresher smoothie, 200, **201**
   Green Apple Delight smoothie, 128
   Healing Greens smoothie, 186
   Mint Julep Sweet Tea smoothie, 206, **207**
   Peachy Kick Start smoothie, **126**, 127
   in preworkout smoothies, 171
   Spiced Apple Core smoothie, 170
Artificial sweeteners, 38
Autumn Bliss smoothie bowl, 235
Avocados
   consistency of smoothies and, 42
   Cream Machine Green Smoothie, 68
   Creamy Banana smoothie bowl, 231
   Dreamy Avocado smoothie bowl, **234**, 235
   Healing Greens smoothie, 186
   Peachy Kick Start smoothie, **126**, 127
   Skinny Mint smoothie, 217
   SPA Cleanser smoothie, 134, **135**
   Veggie-Licious smoothie, 210

B

Baby kale, 36
Baby spinach, 36
Bags, labeling, 47
Bananas
   Açaí Smoothie Bowl smoothie, 232, **233**
   Autumn Bliss smoothie bowl, 235

Banana Berry Blast smoothie, **74**, 75, 75
Banana Mylkshake smoothie, 154
Banana Spice smoothie, 182, **183**
Banana Split smoothie, 154, **155**
Beginner's Luck smoothie, 57, 59
Berry Blastoff! smoothie, 152, **153**
Berry Power Bar smoothie, 173
Carrot Cake smoothie bowl, **238**, 239
Cinnamon Roll smoothie, **216**, 217
Citrus Maca Recharge smoothie, 127
consistency of smoothies and, 42
Cream Machine Green Smoothie, 68
Creamy Banana smoothie bowl, 231
Figgy Pudding smoothie, 218, **219**
Fit Fuel smoothie, **172**, 173
freezing, 43
frozen, 37
Gettin' Figgy with It smoothie, 193
Glowing Green Healer smoothie, 134, **135**
Green Apple Delight smoothie, 128
Green Goblin smoothie, 159
Green Hulk smoothie, 178
Happy Monkey smoothie, 160
improving smoothie taste using, 48
Kale-Licious smoothie, **176,** 177
Mango Orange Madness smoothie, 67
Mexican Hot Chocolate smoothie, 222,
   223
Morning Jump Start smoothie, 170
Peach Party smoothie, **158**, 159
Pineapple Banana Bliss smoothie, 123
Pineapple Upside Down Cake smoothie, 63
Pinky Pie Punch smoothie, **156**, 157
Popeye's Greensicles, 162
in postworkout smoothies, 175
in preworkout smoothies, 171
Pumpkin Pecan Pie smoothie, **224**, 225
Purple Power Healer smoothie, 190, **191**
Rainbow Love smoothie bowl, 240, **241**

Rawkin' Multilayered Tutti-Frutti Pops, **164**, 165
Red Hot Love smoothie bowl, 231
ripeness of, 37
Simple Cherry smoothie, **112**, 113
Simple Citrus smoothie, 114, **115**
Simple Mango smoothie, 118, **119**
Simple Monkey smoothie, **112**, 113
Simple Pineapple smoothie, 110
Skinny Mint smoothie, 217
Spiced Apple Core smoothie, 170
substitutes for, 37
Tangerine Tang smoothie, 131
Tutti-Frutti Pops, 165
Very Berry Citrus smoothie, 64
Basil, 98, **99**
Beets
    Pinky Pie Punch smoothie, **156**, 157
    Red Velvet smoothie, 214, **215**
    Up Beet smoothie, **202**, 203
Beginner's Luck smoothie, **56**, 57, **58**, <u>59</u>
Bell pepper. *See* Peppers
Benefits of green smoothies, 9–10
Berkey countertop water-filter system, 23
Berries. *See also specific berries*
    Açaí Smoothie Bowl smoothie, 232, **233**
    Banana Berry Blast smoothie, 75
    Berry Blastoff! smoothie, 152, **153**
    Berry Power Bar smoothie, 173
    frozen, 61
    high amount of, when to consume, <u>30</u>
    seeds from, 74
    Simple Berry smoothie, 117
    washing, 102
Bitter greens, 32
Bitterness, removing, 41
Black & Decker Fusion Blade blender, 19
Blackberries
    Banana Berry Blast smoothie, 75
    Kiwi Berry Glow smoothie, 138, **139**
    Purple Power Healer smoothie, 190, **191**
Blanching greens, 34
Blenders
    choosing, 16, 19
    cleaning, 20, **21**
    vs. juicers, <u>18</u>
    packing, 26–27
    refurbished, <u>16</u>

    regular vs. high-speed, **19**
    spinning of, aiding, 20
Blendtec blenders, 16
Bloating, <u>30</u>
Blueberries
    Banana Berry Blast smoothie, 75
    Berry Blastoff! smoothie, 152, **153**
    Blue Lavender Ice Cream smoothie, **220**, 221
    Blue Steel smoothie, 174
    Field of Greens smoothie, **208**, 209
    Kale-Licious smoothie, **176,** 177
    in postworkout smoothies, <u>175</u>
    Rainbow Love smoothie bowl, 240, **241**
    Refresh Mint smoothie, 141
    Rise and Shine smoothie, 124, **125**
    Very Berry Citrus smoothie, 64
Blue Lavender Ice Cream smoothie, **220**, 221
Blue Steel smoothie, 174
Bowel movements, 10
Breakfast, <u>30</u>
Breville Hemisphere blenders, 16
Brita faucet-filtration system, 23
Broccoli
    Field of Greens smoothie, **208**, 209
    Healing Greens smoothie, 186
Brown rice, Homemade Nut-Free Milk, 248, **249**
Budgeting, 44, <u>45</u>
Bulk shopping, 44

C

Cabbage
    Citrus Cold Recovery smoothie, 186, **187**
    Purple Power Healer smoothie, 190, **191**
Cacao, **92**, 93
Calories, 9
Cantaloupe, Southern Charm smoothie, **148**, 149
Carmel Cashew Delight smoothie, **130**, 131
Carrots
    Carrot Cake smoothie bowl, **238**, 239
    softening, 73
    Southern Charm smoothie, **148**, 149
    Strawberry Carrot Cooler smoothie, 72
    Veggie-Licious smoothie, 210
Casein, <u>40</u>
Cashews, 90
    Carmel Cashew Delight smoothie, **130**, 131

Celery
   Cool Greens smoothie, **208**, 209
   Dreamy Avocado smoothie bowl, **234**, 235
   Veggie Cocktail smoothie, 210
   Watermelon Fresca smoothie, **184**, 185
Chard. *See also* Swiss chard, Morning Jump Start
      smoothie, 170
Cherries
   Banana Split smoothie, 154, **155**
   Cherry Quinoa Bowl smoothie bowl, 240
   Fruit Cocktail smoothie, 160
   Pineapple Upside Down Cake smoothie, 63
   Simple Cherry smoothie, 113
   Trail Mix smoothie, 178
   Up Beet smoothie, **202**, 203
Chewing green smoothies, 85
Chia seeds, 42, 84, **85**
Chlorella, 94
Chlorophyll, 94
Chocolate. *See* Cacao
Chunks, eliminating, 27, 35
Cilantro, 98, **99**
Cinnamon, 96, **96**, 97
   Cinnamon Roll smoothie, **216**, 217
Citrus, 34. *See also* Lemon juice; Lime juice;
      Nectarines; Oranges
   Citrus Cold Recovery smoothie, 186, **187**
   Citrus Crush smoothie, 76, **77**
   Citrus Maca Recharge smoothie, 127
Cleaning blenders, **21**
Clementines
   Carrot Cake smoothie bowl, **238**, 239
   Pinky Pie Punch smoothie, **156**, 157
Coconut milk, Homemade Coconut Milk, **246**,
      247
Coconut oil, 171
Coconut water, 67, 175
Colds, 10
Collard greens, Southern Charm smoothie, **148**,
      149
Color of smoothies, 37
Compost, 24
Consistency of smoothies, 42, 48
Conversion guide, 260
Cool as a Cucumber smoothie, **136**, 137
Cool Greens smoothie, **208**, 209
Costs, 44, 45
Counting calories, 9
Cramps, 37

Cranberries, Autumn Bliss smoothie bowl, 235
Cravings, 4, 6, 10, 30
Cream Machine Green Smoothie, 20, 68, **69**
Creamy Banana smoothie bowl, 231
Cucumbers
   Cucumber Lassi smoothie, **188**, 189
   Dreamy Avocado smoothie bowl, **234**, 235
   Gazpacho smoothie bowl, 236, **237**
   Lean Green Cleanser smoothie, 198, **199**
Cuisinart Hand Blender, 19
Cuppow lids, 23
Cutting up ingredients, 20

D

Dairy, 6, 40
Dairy alternatives, 60
Daisy cut lids, 23
Dandelion greens, Cool Greens smoothie, **208**,
      209
Defrosting frozen fruit, 41
Destemming greens, 35, 41
Detoxstar smoothie, 204, **205**
Diets, 4–6
Dinner, 30
Dreamy Avocado smoothie bowl, **234**, 235
Dry ingredients, packing into blender, 26–27

E

Earthy flavor greens, 32

F

Fat (body), 86
Fat (dietary), 10, 30
Fennel, Florida Fennel Refresher, 200, **201**
Fiber, 10
   benefits of, 38
   bloating and, 30
   when blending vs. juicing, 18
Field of Green smoothie, **208**, 209
Figs
   Figgy Pudding smoothie, 218, **219**
   Gettin' Figgy with It smoothie, 193
Fit Fuel smoothie, **172**, 173
Flavor
   of greens, 32
   of smoothies, improving, 41, 48

Flaxseed oil, 89
Flaxseeds, 84, **85**
Florida Fennel Refresher smoothie, 200, **201**
Flus, 10
Focus, 10
Food sensitivities, 6, 40
Fountain of Youth smoothie, 138
Freezing
    fruits, 43, 47
    greens, 34, 47, 70
    smoothies, 28, 48
Fridges, storing smoothies in, 28, 101
Frozen fruit, 20, 37, 42
    berries, 61
    defrosting, 41
Fructose, 38
Fruit Cocktail smoothie, 160
Fruit flies, 39
Fruits. *See also specific fruits*
    freezing, 47
    frozen, 20, 37, 42
    high amount of, when to consume, 30
    improving smoothie taste using, 48
    low-glycemic, 38
    number of servings in smoothie, 28
    organic, 105
    packing into blender, 26–27
    pesticides on, 105
    precut, 37
    ripeness of, 37, 41
    sugar in, 38
    washing, 47, 102

G

Gazpacho smoothie bowl, 236, **237**
Georgia Peach Pie smoothie, 226, **227**
Gettin' Figgy with It smoothie, 193
Ginger, **96**, 97, 97
    Ginger Berry Mojito smoothie, 200, **201**
    Mango Ginger Zinger smoothie, 124
Glowing Green Healer smoothie, 134, **135**
Gluten, 6, 40
Goji berries, 94
Grapefruits, Oh My Grapefruit smoothie, 128,
    129
Grapes
    Citrus Crush smoothie, 76
    Cool as a Cucumber smoothie, **136**, 137

Fruit Cocktail smoothie, 160
    Peach Coconut Dream smoothie, 71
    Simple Greens smoothie, **116**, 117
Green Apple Delight smoothie, 128
Green Goblin smoothie, 159
Green Hulk smoothie, 178, **179**
Greens. *See also specific greens*
    blanching, 34
    destemming, 35
    freezing, 34
    hard-core, 31, 80
    measuring, 32, 65
    organic, 105
    pesticides on, 76, 105
    variety of, 32
    washing, 47, 102
    wilted, 34
    young, 36
Green Smoothie Bowl Formula, 230
Green smoothies
    amount to drink, 4, 28
    benefits of, 9–10
    chewing, 85
    color of, 37
    combining with meal, 30
    consistency of, 42, 48
    creamy, 42
    flavor of, improving, 41, 48
    on the go, 101
    as meal replacement, 42
    motivation for making/drinking, 52
    serving sizes, 28
    storing, 28
    vitamins and nutrients in, 9
    when to drink, 30
Green tea
    Mango Ginger Zinger smoothie, 124
    Mint Julep Sweet Tea smoothie,
        206, **207**
Ground red pepper, **96**, 97

H

"hangry," 83
Happy Melon smoothie bowl, 232
Happy Monkey smoothie, 160
Hard-core greens, 31, 80
Hard ingredients, 20
Hemp hearts, 84, **85**, 175

Herbs. *See also specific herbs*
   boosting green smoothies with, 98
   ice cubes made with, 49
Homemade Almond Milk, 244, **245**
Homemade Almond Nut Butter, 252, **253**
Homemade Coconut Milk, **246**, 247
Homemade Coconut Whipped Cream,
      256, **257**
Homemade Nut-Free Milk, 248, **249**
Homemade Vanilla Extract, **254**, 255
Honeydew melon
   Cool as a Cucumber smoothie, **136**, 137
   Glowing Green Healer smoothie,
      134, **135**
   Simple Melon smoothie, 114
Hotels, fridges in, 101

I

Ice cubes, 48, 49
Infections, 10, 40
Inflammation, 10, 40

J

Jars. *See* Mason jars
Jen's Coconut Granola, **250**, 251
Juicers, 18

K

Kale
   baby kale, 36
   Beginner's Luck smoothie, 59
   Cool Greens smoothie, **208**, 209
   destemming, 35
   Fountain of Youth smoothie, 138
   Healing Greens smoothie, 186
   Kale-Licious smoothie, **176,** 177
   Kalifornia Sunshine smoothie, **122**, 123
   Lean Green Cleanser smoothie, 198, **199**
   pesticides on, 76
   Pineapple Banana Bliss smoothie, 123
   Pineapple Mojito smoothie, 146, **147**
   Refresh Mint smoothie, 141
   Tropical Turmeric Cleanser smoothie,
      140, 141
   Veggie Cocktail smoothie, 210
   Vitamin C Fiesta smoothie, 193
Kalifornia Sunshine smoothie, **122**, 123

Kiwifruit
   Glowing Green Healer smoothie, 134, **135**
   Kiwi Berry Glow smoothie, 138, **139**
   Mango Ginger Zinger smoothie, 124
   Simple Colada smoothie, 110, **111**
   Tropical Beauty smoothie, 145
   Vitamin C Fiesta smoothie, 193

L

Labels, 47
Leafy greens. *See* Greens
Lean Green Cleanser smoothie, 198, **199**
Lemon juice, 28, 34, 41
   Blue Lavender Ice Cream smoothie, **220**, 221
   Citrus Cold Recovery smoothie, 186, **187**
   Cool as a Cucumber smoothie, 137
   Cool Greens smoothie, **208**, 209
   Creamy Banana smoothie bowl, 231
   Cucumber Lassi smoothie, 188, 189
   Dreamy Avocado smoothie bowl, **234**, 235
   Florida Fennel Refresher smoothie, 200, **201**
   Gazpacho smoothie bowl, 236, **237**
   Ginger Berry Mojito smoothie, 200, **201**
   Healing Greens smoothie, 186
   Mint Julep Sweet Tea smoothie, 206, **207**
   Sweet Turmeric Twister smoothie, 190, **191**
   Tropical Turmeric Cleanser smoothie, **140**, 141
   Veggie-Licious smoothie, 210
Lids, of Mason jars, 23
Lime juice, 34
   Agua Fresca Detox smoothie, 204, **205**
   Dreamy Avocado smoothie bowl, **234**, 235
   Glowing Green Healer smoothie, 134, **135**
   Lean Green Cleanser smoothie, 198, **199**
   Peachy Kick Start smoothie, **126**, 127
   Pineapple Mojito smoothie, 146, **147**
   Sweet Relief smoothie, **176**, 177
   Tropical Mango-Rita smoothie, 194, **195**
   Veggie Cocktail smoothie, 210
   Watermelon Mojito smoothie, **184**, 185

M

Maca powder, 94
   Citrus Maca Recharge smoothie, 127
Magic Rawkstar smoothie, 31
Mangoes
   Beginner's Luck smoothie, **56**, 57, **58**, 59
   Blue Steel smoothie, 174

Cream Machine Green Smoothie, 68
Fountain of Youth smoothie, 138
Kalifornia Sunshine smoothie, **122**, 123
Mango Ginger Zinger smoothie, 124
Mango Orange Madness smoothie, **66**, 67
Pink Flamango smoothie, 60
Simple Apricot smoothie, 118
Simple Mango smoothie, 118, **119**
Southern Charm smoothie, **148**, 149
Thanksgiving in Your Mouth smoothie, **224**, 225
Tropical Beauty smoothie, 145
Tropical Mango-Rita smoothie, 194, **195**
Tropical Turmeric Cleanser smoothie, **140**, 141
Watermelon Mojito smoothie, **184**, 185
Mason jars, 23
    labeling, 47
    traveling with, 101
Meals
    combining smoothies with, 30
    smoothies as replacements for, 42, 83
Measuring greens, 32, 65
Melon. See Cantaloupe; Honeydew melon; Watermelon
Mexican Hot Chocolate smoothie, 222, **223**
Mighty Matcha Mango smoothie, 168, **169**
Milks. See Dairy; Nut milks
Mint, 98
    Cucumber Lassi smoothie, **188**, 189
    Ginger Berry Mojito smoothie, 200, **201**
    Kiwi Berry Glow smoothie, 138, **139**
    Mint Julep Sweet Tea smoothie, 206, **207**
    Pineapple Mojito smoothie, 146, **147**
    Refresh Mint smoothie, 141
    Skinny Mint smoothie, 217
    Watermelon Mojito smoothie, **184**, 185
Money, saving, 44, 45
Mood swings, 37
Morning Jump Start smoothie, 170
Motivation for making/drinking smoothies, 52

N

Nectarines, Morning Jump Start smoothie, 170
Nut butters
    Homemade Almond Nut Butter, 252, **253**
    in postworkout smoothies, 175
    in preworkout smoothies, 171

Nut milks, 244–47
    Homemade Almond Milk, 244, **245**
    Homemade Coconut Milk, **246**, 247
NutriBullet Pro blender, 16, 19
Nutrients, 9, 261–63
Nuts, soaking, 90, 90, **91**. See also specific nuts

O

Oats, 87
    Berry Power Bar smoothie, 173
    Green Apple Delight smoothie, 128
    Homemade Nut-Free Milk, 248, **249**
    Jen's Coconut Granola, **250**, 251
    Morning Jump Start smoothie, 170
    in preworkout smoothies, 171
    Trail Mix smoothie, 178
Oh My Grapefruit smoothie, 128, **129**
Oil. See Coconut oil; Flaxseed oil
Orange juice, 66
Oranges
    Citrus Cold Recovery smoothie, 186, **187**
    Citrus Crush smoothie, 76
    Citrus Maca Recharge smoothie, 127
    Field of Greens smoothie, **208**, 209
    Florida Fennel Refresher smoothie, 200, **201**
    Green Goblin smoothie, 159
    Kalifornia Sunshine smoothie, **122**, 123
    Lean Green Cleanser smoothie, 198, **199**
    Mango Orange Madness smoothie, 67
    Oh My Grapefruit smoothie, 128, **129**
    Papaya Sunrise smoothie, 142, **143**
    Peach Party smoothie, **158**, 159
    peeling, 114
    Pinky Pie Punch smoothie, **156**, 157
    Popeye's Greensicles, 162
    in postworkout smoothies, 175
    Purple Power Healer smoothie, 190, **191**
    Rainbow Love smoothie bowl, 240, **241**
    Simple Berry smoothie, 117
    Simple Citrus smoothie, 114, **115**
    sweetness of, 41
    Sweet Relief smoothie, **176,** 177
    Tropical Mango-Rita smoothie, 194, **195**
    Up Beet smoothie, **202**, 203
    Very Berry Citrus smoothie, 64
    Vitamin C Fiesta smoothie, 193
Organic fruits and vegetables, 105
Oster Counterforms 7-Speed blender, 19
Oxidation, 23, 28

P

Packing blenders, 26–27
Papaya Sunrise smoothie, 142, **143**
Paper straws, 23
Parsley, 98, **99**
Peaches
    Agua Fresca Detox smoothie, 204, **205**
    Detoxstar smoothie, 204, **205**
    Fit Fuel smoothie, **172**, 173
    Fruit Cocktail smoothie, 160
    Georgia Peach Pie smoothie, 226, **227**
    Green Hulk smoothie, 178
    Mint Julep Sweet Tea smoothie, 206, **207**
    Peach Coconut Dream smoothie, **70**, 71
    Peach Party smoothie, **158**, 159
    Peach Pear Refresher smoothie, 198, **199**
    Peachy Kick Start smoothie, **126**, 127
    Radiant Cooler smoothie, 145
    Rawkin' Multilayered Tutti-Frutti Pops, **164**,
        165
    Tutti-Frutti Pops, 165
Pears
    Banana Mylkshake smoothie, 154
    Carmel Cashew Delight smoothie, **130**, 131
    Cool Greens smoothie, **208**, 209
    Fruit Cocktail smoothie, 160
    Lean Green Cleanser smoothie, 198, **199**
    Peach Pear Refresher smoothie, 198, **199**
    Rise and Shine smoothie, 124, **125**
    Simple Greens smoothie, **116**, 117
    Toasted Coconut Almond Fudge smoothie, 226
Pecans, Pumpkin Pecan Pie smoothie, **224**, 225
Pepper, ground red, **96**, 97
Peppers
    Gazpacho smoothie bowl, 236, **237**
    Healing Greens smoothie, 186
    Mexican Hot Chocolate smoothie, 222, **223**
    Veggie Cocktail smoothie, 210
    Vitamin C Fiesta smoothie, 193
Peppery flavor greens, 32
Peruvian ginseng, 94
Pesticides, 76, 105
Pineapple
    Agua Fresca Detox smoothie, 204, **205**
    Beginner's Luck smoothie, 57, 59
    Carrot Cake smoothie bowl, **238**, 239
    Citrus Cold Recovery smoothie, 186, **187**
    Citrus Crush smoothie, 76
    Fit Fuel smoothie, **172**, 173
    Fountain of Youth smoothie, 138
    Fruit Cocktail smoothie, 160
    Green Goblin smoothie, 159
    Kale-Licious smoothie, **176,** 177
    Kalifornia Sunshine smoothie, **122**, 123
    Mango Ginger Zinger smoothie, 124
    Oh My Grapefruit smoothie, 128, **129**
    Papaya Sunrise smoothie, 142, **143**
    Pineapple Banana Bliss smoothie, 123
    Pineapple Mojito smoothie, 146, **147**
    Pineapple Upside Down Cake smoothie, **62**, 63
    in postworkout smoothies, 175
    Rawkin' Multilayered Tutti-Frutti Pops, **164**, 165
    Refresh Mint smoothie, 141
    Simple Colada smoothie, 110, **111**
    Simple Melon smoothie, 114
    Simple Pineapple smoothie, 110
    Southern Charm smoothie, **148**, 149
    SPA Cleanser smoothie, 134, **135**
    Strawberry Carrot Cooler smoothie, 72
    Sweet Relief smoothie, **176,** 177
    Sweet Turmeric Twister smoothie, 190, **191**
    Tangerine Tang smoothie, 131
    Tropical Beauty smoothie, 145
    Tropical Mango-Rita smoothie, 194, **195**
    Tutti-Frutti Pops, 165
    Up Beet smoothie, **202**, 203
    Watermelon Fresca smoothie, **184**, 185
Pink Flamango smoothie, 60, **61**
Pinky Pie Punch smoothie, **156**, 157
Planning, importance of, 52
Popsicles, 162–65
Potatoes. *See* Sweet potatoes
Precut fruit, 37
Preparing ahead of time, 44, 47
Processed sugars, 6, 38, 40
Produce. *See* Fruits; Greens
Protein, 30
Pulp, 18
Pumpkin
    Autumn Bliss smoothie bowl, 235
    Pumpkin Pecan Pie smoothie, **224**, 225
Purple Power Healer smoothie, 190, **191**

Q

Quinoa, 87
    Cherry Quinoa Bowl smoothie bowl, 240

R

Radiant Cooler smoothie, 145
Rainbow Love smoothie bowl, 240, **241**
Raspberries
    Banana Berry Blast smoothie, 75
    Berry Power Bar smoothie, 173
    Citrus Maca Recharge smoothie, 127
    Gettin' Figgy with It smoothie, 193
    Rawkin' Multilayered Tutti-Frutti Pops, **164**, 165
    Red Hot Love smoothie bowl, 231
    Tutti-Frutti Pops, 165
Rawkin' Multilayered Tutti-Frutti Pops, **164**, 165
Red bell pepper. *See* Peppers
Red Hot Love smoothie bowl, 231
Red pepper, ground, **96**, 97
Red Velvet smoothie, 214, **215**
Refined sugars, 6, 38, 40
Refresh Mint smoothie, 141
Refrigerators, storing smoothies in, 28, 101
Refurbished blenders, 16
Reusable straws, 23
Rice, Homemade Nut-Free Milk, 248, **249**
Ripeness of fruit, 37, 41
Rise and Shine smoothie, 124, **125**
Romaine
    Carrot Cake smoothie bowl, **238**, 239
    Gazpacho smoothie bowl, 236, **237**
Root vegetables, washing, 102

S

SAD, 40
Seasonal shopping, 44
Seeds. *See also specific seeds*
    from berries, 74
    soaking, 90, 90
Sensitivities to foods, 6, 40
Serving sizes, 28
Shopping
    bulk, 44
    lists for, 52, 53
    seasonal, 44
Sickness, avoiding, 10, 40
Silverbeet. *See* Swiss chard
Simple Apricot smoothie, 118
Simple Berry smoothie, 117
Simple Cherry smoothie, **112**, 113
Simple Citrus smoothie, 114, **115**
Simple Colada smoothie, 110, **111**
Simple Greens smoothie, **116**, 117
Simple Mango smoothie, 118, **119**
Simple Melon smoothie, 114
Simple Monkey smoothie, **112**, 113
Simple Pineapple smoothie, 110
Skinny Mint smoothie, 217
Smoothies. *See* Green smoothies
Soaking
    nuts, 90, 90, **91**
    seeds, 90, 90
Soda, 9
Southern Charm smoothie, **148**, 149
SPA Cleanser smoothie, 134, **135**
Spiced Apple Core smoothie, 170
Spices, **96**, 97
Spills, avoiding, 23
Spinach
    Açaí Smoothie Bowl smoothie, 232, **233**
    Agua Fresca Detox smoothie, 204, **205**
    Autumn Bliss smoothie bowl, 235
    baby spinach, 36
    Banana Berry Blast smoothie, 75
    Banana Mylkshake smoothie, 154
    Banana Spice smoothie, 182, **183**
    Banana Split smoothie, 154, **155**
    Beginner's Luck smoothie, **56**, 57, **58**, 59
    Berry Blastoff! smoothie, 152, **153**
    Berry Power Bar smoothie, 173
    Blue Lavender Ice Cream smoothie, **220**, 221
    Blue Steel smoothie, 174
    Carmel Cashew Delight smoothie, **130**, 131
    Cinnamon Roll smoothie, **216**, 217
    Citrus Crush smoothie, 76
    Citrus Maca Recharge smoothie, 127
    Cool as a Cucumber smoothie, **136**, 137
    Cream Machine Green Smoothie, 68
    Creamy Banana smoothie bowl, 231
    Cucumber Lassi smoothie, **188**, 189
    Detoxstar smoothie, 204, **205**
    Dreamy Avocado smoothie bowl, **234**, 235
    Field of Greens smoothie, **208**, 209
    Figgy Pudding smoothie, 218, **219**
    Fit Fuel smoothie, **172**, 173
    Florida Fennel Refresher smoothie, 200, **201**
    Fountain of Youth smoothie, 138
    freezing, 70

Spinach (*cont.*)
Fruit Cocktail smoothie, 160
Georgia Peach Pie smoothie, 226, **227**
Gettin' Figgy with It smoothie, 193
Ginger Berry Mojito smoothie, 200, **201**
Glowing Green Healer smoothie, 134, **135**
Green Apple Delight smoothie, 128
Green Goblin smoothie, 159
Happy Melon smoothie bowl, 232
Happy Monkey smoothie, 160
Kiwi Berry Glow smoothie, 138, **139**
Mango Orange Madness smoothie, 67
measuring, 65
Mexican Hot Chocolate smoothie, 222, **223**
Mighty Matcha Mango smoothie, 168, **169**
Mint Julep Sweet Tea smoothie, 206, **207**
Oh My Grapefruit smoothie, 128, **129**
Papaya Sunrise smoothie, 142, **143**
Peach Coconut Dream smoothie, 71
Peach Party smoothie, **158**, 159
pesticides on, 76
Pineapple Upside Down Cake smoothie, 63
Pink Flamango smoothie, 60
Pinky Pie Punch smoothie, **156**, 157
Popeye's Greensicles, 162
Pumpkin Pecan Pie smoothie, **224**, 225
Radiant Cooler smoothie, 145
Rainbow Love smoothie bowl, 240, **241**
Rawkin' Multilayered Tutti-Frutti Pops, **164**, 165
Red Hot Love smoothie bowl, 231
Red Velvet smoothie, 214, **215**
Simple Apricot smoothie, 118
Simple Berry smoothie, 117
Simple Cherry smoothie, 113
Simple Citrus smoothie, 114, **115**
Simple Colada smoothie, 110, **111**
Simple Greens smoothie, **116**, 117
Simple Mango smoothie, 118, **119**
Simple Melon smoothie, 114
Simple Monkey smoothie, **112**, 113
Simple Pineapple smoothie, 110
Skinny Mint smoothie, 217
SPA Cleanser smoothie, 134, **135**
Spiced Apple Core smoothie, 170
Strawberry Carrot Cooler smoothie, 72
Sweet Relief smoothie, **176,** 177
Sweet Turmeric Twister smoothie, 190, **191**
taste of, 32

Thanksgiving in Your Mouth smoothie, **224**, 225
Toasted Coconut Almond Fudge smoothie, 226
Trail Mix smoothie, 178
Tropical Beauty smoothie, 145
Tropical Mango-Rita smoothie, 194, **195**
Tutti-Frutti Pops, 165
Up Beet smoothie, **202**, 203
Veggie-Licious smoothie, 210
Very Berry Citrus smoothie, 64
Watermelon Fresca smoothie, **184**, 185
Spirulina, 94
Stainless steel straws, 23
Standard American Diet (SAD), 40
Starter formula, 31
Stems, removing, 35, 41
Stomach aches, 6
Storage, 28, 47
Strawberries
Berry Blastoff! smoothie, 152, **153**
Berry Power Bar smoothie, 173
Detoxstar smoothie, 204, **205**
Ginger Berry Mojito smoothie, 200, **201**
Happy Melon smoothie bowl, 232
Pink Flamango smoothie, 60
Pinky Pie Punch smoothie, **156**, 157
Radiant Cooler smoothie, 145
Rainbow Love smoothie bowl, 240, **241**
Rawkin' Multilayered Tutti-Frutti Pops, **164**, 165
Red Hot Love smoothie bowl, 231
Red Velvet smoothie, 214, **215**
Strawberry Carrot Cooler smoothie, 72, **73**
Tutti-Frutti Pops, 165
Very Berry Citrus smoothie, 64
Vitamin C Fiesta smoothie, 193
Straws, 23
Subtle greens, 32
Sugars
in fruit, 38
processed/refined, 6, 38, 40
Superfoods, 44, 83, **92**, 93–94
Sweeteners, artificial, 38
Sweetness, reducing, 34
Sweet potatoes
in postworkout smoothies, 175
Sweet Relief smoothie, **176,** 177

Thanksgiving in Your Mouth smoothie,
    224, 225
washing, 102
Sweet Relief smoothie, **176,** 177
Sweet Turmeric Twister smoothie, 190, **191**
Swiss chard
    Cherry Quinoa Bowl smoothie bowl, 240
    Green Hulk smoothie, 178
    Mango Ginger Zinger smoothie, 124
    Peach Pear Refresher smoothie, 198, **199**
    Peachy Kick Start smoothie, **126**, 127
    Rise and Shine smoothie, 124, **125**
    Tangerine Tang smoothie, 131
    Watermelon Mojito smoothie, **184**, 185

T

Tangerine Tang smoothie, 131
Thanksgiving in Your Mouth smoothie, **224**, 225
Thinning out smoothie, 48
Time, saving, 44
Toasted Coconut Almond Fudge smoothie, 226
Tomatoes
    Gazpacho smoothie bowl, 236, **237**
    Healing Greens smoothie, 186
    Veggie Cocktail smoothie, 210
    Veggie-Licious smoothie, 210
Tote bags, 24
Toxins, 32
Trail Mix smoothie, 178, **179**
Traveling, 101
Tropical Beauty smoothie, 145
Tropical Mango Rita smoothie, 194, **195**
Tropical Turmeric Cleanser smoothie, **140**, 141
Turmeric, **96**, 97
    Sweet Turmeric Twister smoothie, 190, **191**
    Tropical Turmeric Cleanser smoothie, **140**, 141
Tutti-Frutti Pops, 165

U

Up Beet smoothie, **202**, 203

V

Vanilla, 96
Vanilla extract, Homemade Vanilla Extract,
    254, 255
Vegetables. *See* Greens
Veggie Cocktail smoothie, 210
Veggie-Licious smoothie, 210
Very Berry Citrus smoothie, 64, **65**
Viruses, 10, 10
Vitamin C Fiesta smoothie, 193
Vitamins, 9, 10, 261–63
Vitamix blenders, 16

W

Washing fruits and vegetables, 47, 102
Water filters, 23
Watermelon
    Fountain of Youth smoothie, 138
    Happy Melon smoothie bowl, 232
    Radiant Cooler smoothie, 145
    Watermelon Fresca smoothie, **184**, 185
    Watermelon Mojito smoothie, **184**, 185
Weight gain, 4
Weight loss, 83
Wheatgrass, 94
Whipped cream, Homemade Coconut Whipped
    Cream, 256, **257**
Wilted greens, 34

Y

Young leafy greens, 36

Notes

Notes

Notes

Notes

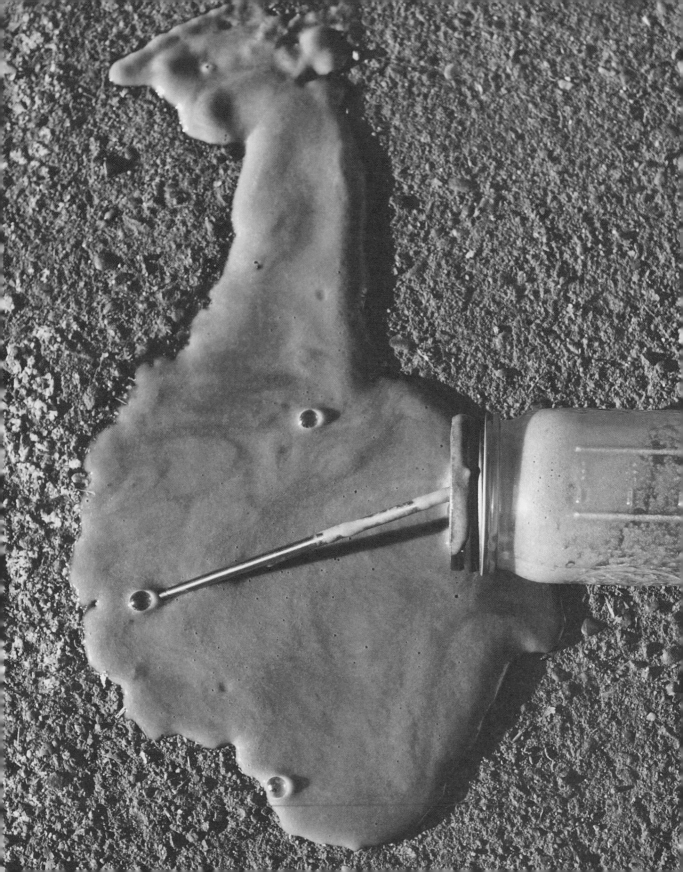